Cognitive Behavioural Therapy
for Chronic Fatigue Syndrome

Chronic fatigue syndrome is a common and disabling condition characterised by fatigue, muscle pain, sleep disturbances and other physical and psychological symptoms that cause a considerable amount of distress and suffering. This book provides a practical guide for clinicians on how to treat chronic fatigue syndrome using cognitive behavioural therapy approaches.

Cognitive Behavioural Therapy for Chronic Fatigue Syndrome attempts to make sense of the illness, and describes how cognitive behavioural therapy can help patients by working with their environment, emotions, and behaviour to improve their physical condition. Topics covered include:

- Principles of cognitive behavioural therapy
- Assessing patients with chronic fatigue syndrome
- Helping patients with emotional issues and other maintenance factors
- Using cognitive behavioural therapy alongside other approaches

Aimed at practitioners, this book will provide essential guidance for cognitive behavioural therapists, physiotherapists, occupational therapists, and other clinicians who work in this rapidly expanding field.

Philip Kinsella is a cognitive behavioural therapist specialising in general hospital liaison work. He has assessed or treated over a hundred patients with chronic fatigue syndrome.

Cognitive Behavioural Therapy for Chronic Fatigue Syndrome

A guide for clinicians

Philip Kinsella

Routledge
Taylor & Francis Group

LONDON AND NEW YORK

First published 2007 by Routledge
27 Church Road, Hove, East Sussex BN3 2FA
Simultaneously published in the USA and Canada
by Routledge
270 Madison Avenue, New York, NY 10016

Routledge is an imprint of the Taylor & Francis Group, an Informa business

© 2007 Philip Kinsella

Typeset in Times by Regent Typesetting, London
Printed and bound in Great Britain by MPG Books Ltd, Bodmin, Cornwall
Paperback cover design by Design Deluxe

This publication has been produced with paper manufactured to strict
environmental standards and with pulp derived from sustainable forests.

British Library Cataloguing in Publication Data
A catalogue record for this book is available from the British Library

Library of Congress Cataloging in Publication Data
Kinsella, Philip, 1957-
    Cognitive behavioural therapy for chronic fatigue syndrome : a guide for
clinicians / Philip Kinsella.
        p. ; cm.
    Includes bibliographical references and index.
    ISBN-13: 978-1-58391-737-4 (hardback)
    ISBN-10: 1-58391-737-3 (hardback)
    ISBN-13: 978-0-415-43612-0 (pbk.)
    ISBN-10: 0-415-43612-5 (pbk.)
    1. Chronic fatigue syndrome--Treatment. 2. Cognitive therapy. 3. Chronic
fatigue syndrome--Treatment. 4. Cognitive therapy. I. Title.
    [DNLM: 1. Fatigue Syndrome, Chronic--therapy. 2. Cognitive Therapy--
methods. WB 146 K51c 2007]
    RB150.F37K55 2007
    616'.0478--dc22
                                            2007003580
/KIN

ISBN: 978-1-58391-737-4 (hbk)
ISBN: 978-0-415-43612-0 (pbk)

Dedicated to my mother, Mrs Anne Kinsella

Contents

Foreword

Chronic fatigue syndrome (CFS) has the reputation of being a peculiar illness. A sense of oddness hangs over the condition, with professionals and lay people 'believing' or 'disbelieving' in its very existence. A multitude of strong but mutually contradictory theories are elaborated about CFS, ranging from psychological interpretations that fail to take account of physical experiences to dogmatic, unevidenced biological theories. Lapp (2000 – quoted in this book) adds a disturbing element to the sense of mystery surrounding CFS by claiming that it belongs to a 'new paradigm… where only specialised probing of the immune, endocrine and central nervous systems reveals evidence of malfunction and disease'.

This can all be deeply confusing and distressing for individuals who are contending with CFS as a daily reality, and Philip Kinsella's book comes as a welcome antidote to such talk. In place of wild overstatements and unsupported generalisations we get an account of CFS that is on the one hand objective and on the other hand person-centred, reflecting the author's long clinical experience of working with affected people. Throughout, the emphasis is on the very real suffering and disabilities of people with CFS. The book provides a practical introduction to cognitive behavioural therapy (CBT), at the same time highlighting principles that can be applied more widely in therapeutic practice.

This book will be helpful for patients as well as for professionals because of the useful insights available in preceding chapters concerning the principles, applications and limitations of CBT. Many health care interventions are presented as occult technologies beyond the grasp of non-specialists, let alone mere patients. By contrast, the whole spirit of CBT encourages collaboration between the therapist and the patient who together co-construct their formulations and strategies. The more the patient can understand the conceptual framework of CBT the better, and through reading this book we are all drawn into such a collaborative process. However, 'do it yourself' CBT is not to be recommended. Cognitive behavioural therapy can be portrayed, especially in the trial literature, as something that can be applied more or less mechanically to a patient, like paint. Philip Kinsella implicitly undermines that misconception, pointing out the subtleties and complexities of CBT, and the ways in which successful work with CFS patients requires generic techniques to be refined specifically for this clientele.

Despite claims to the contrary, CFS does not belong in a new paradigm, and patients might be reassured if more of them realised that the principles of CBT are applicable in a very wide range of medical conditions, where effective outcomes depend on a combination of biological and non-biological strategies.

C. D. Ward
Professor of Rehabilitation Medicine, Derby City Hospital, UK
Network Coordinator, CFS Clinical Network, East Midlands, UK

Preface

Chronic fatigue syndrome (CFS) is a common, disabling and controversial condition. It is characterised by fatigue, muscle pain, sleep disturbances and other physical and psychological symptoms. It often presents at the interface between psychological and physical health systems, and is viewed to be difficult to manage and treat (Cox 2000). Undoubtedly it causes a considerable amount of distress and suffering.

Cognitive behavioural therapy (CBT) is a treatment that is now accepted as helpful for a wide range of disorders including panic disorder, agoraphobia, mild to moderate depression and many others (Simos 2002). The therapy aims to look at the link between the environment, the person's thinking, their emotions, their physiology and their behaviour. A detailed assessment leads to a formulation, shared with the patient, that attempts to make sense of these links. Longer term goals are then agreed, and a variety of treatment strategies are used, including challenging negative thoughts and beliefs, helping patients change behaviour, meditation and relaxation, and problem solving. Outcomes in terms of patient functioning and level of symptoms are carefully measured. The treatment is conducted with an awareness of the importance of the therapeutic relationship. Cognitive behavioural therapy is being used increasingly by health professionals throughout the world, being viewed as effective, popular with patients, and highly practical.

There is unfortunately no treatment that is absolutely effective in CFS, however in the 1990s CBT theorists developed models of this condition (see Surawy, Hackman, Hawton and Sharpe 1995) and various trials have been conducted that have shown CBT and graded exercise to be helpful (Kinsella 2002). This book will be based on the author's experience of using CBT with adult CFS patients. He has seen over a hundred patients and treated 50–60 using CBT. He spent six months working in the CFS Research Unit at Kings College Hospital in London, where these treatments were developed, and now works in a Psychological Medicine Service. The book is a treatment manual that will guide Cognitive Behavioural Therapists, clinicians such as occupational therapists and physiotherapists, and patients in the treatment of these problems in adults. Controversies around CFS are addressed, but the focus is on practical help, as these controversies have been much discussed elsewhere (Wessely, Hotopf and Sharpe 1998). Cognitive behavioural therapy is not presented as a cure for CFS, but more realistically, as something that can be helpful. Clinical case histories and actual treatment examples will be used to illustrate key points.

The book will start by outlining the principles of CBT, and then a CBT model of CFS will be described. A section on assessment of patients is followed by detailed chapters on treatment approaches. After that, a patient who is quite badly affected by the condition gives her account, and there is an author commentary. Integrating CBT with other approaches and developing services make up the remainder of the book.

The UK government released 8.5 million pounds over the years 2004–2006 for the treatment of CFS (www.nhs.uk). Also the provisional UK National Institute for Clinical Excellence (NICE 2006) guidelines have been made available on the web, as the book was being finished. (This provisional publication is a stage that allows final comments to be made before final publication.) The guidelines describe the general principles of care, the issue of making a diagnosis, management of the condition, and the care of the severely affected. The guideline emphasises the importance of taking individual needs and preferences into consideration, good communication, and the provision of evidence based information. It recommends that when the person's goal is to return to normal activities then the therapies of first choice should be CBT or graded exercise therapy. If these approaches are not appropriate then elements of them such as activity management, sleep management and relaxation should be offered.

Hopefully with this much-needed increase in resource, and the publication of the NICE guidelines, the material in the book will be useful for clinicians who want a practical guide. The author has attempted to make it compatible with the NICE guidelines, and accessible to psychological therapists, and to clinicians such as occupational therapists and physiotherapists who wish to include the CBT approach in their work. Chapters 2 and 3 on understanding CBT and assessing patients for it may be of less interest to those experienced in CBT.

Note on fibromyalgia

Fibromyalgia is a chronic musculoskeletal disorder. The diagnosis is made (usually by rheumatologists), by the identification of pain and hypersensitivity at specific 'tender points'. However, as Wolfe, Smythe, Yunus, Bennet, Bombadier, Goldenberg et al (1990) show, fibromyalgia patients also describe chronic fatigue (78.2 per cent), sleep disturbances (75.6 per cent), stiffness (76.2 per cent), headaches 54.3 per cent), irritable bowel (35.7 per cent), depression and anxiety (44.9 per cent). One can see that there is overlap between these conditions and it has been argued that they are the same condition (Turk and Ellis 2003), or that the same mechanisms drive them. Although this book is primarily about treating CFS the approaches could easily be applied to fibromyalgia, and this author is not aware that any of them would be contra-indicated.

Acknowledgements

I would like to thank various colleagues who have helped me think about chronic fatigue syndrome: Trudie Chalder, Mary Burgess, Alison Wearden, Chris Atha, Rachel Atherton and others. Also, colleagues in Psychological Medicine in Nottingham, and the managers of Nottinghamshire Health Care Trust have been helpful and supportive. I would like to thank the patients I have seen over the years.

Chapter 1

Understanding chronic fatigue syndrome from a cognitive behavioural perspective

This chapter covers:

- How chronic fatigue syndrome (CFS) presents to the health system and how it is defined
- A description of the cognitive behavioural therapy (CBT) model of CFS
- An explanation of how this model has been developed historically, and of how it is supported by research evidence and clinical experience
- Criticisms of the CBT model

A description of CFS

Chronic fatigue syndrome is a complex and disabling condition characterised by persistent and unexplained physical and mental fatigue, and other symptoms as described below (Jason, Fennell and Taylor 2003). Patients will present themselves, usually to their general practitioner (GP), with symptoms of particularly fatigue, but also pain, poor concentration, poor sleep, and sometimes odd symptoms such as heat and cold intolerance. These symptoms may have been preceded by a physical illness or a period of stress. Little is found on physical examination, symptoms are usually viewed as viral by the GP, but patients get frustrated that their symptoms do not clear up as would be expected. Aside from the great unpleasantness of these symptoms, they can make it difficult for the person to function at their normal level in terms of family life and work. They can be frustrated by this and the fact that there is no obvious medical cure, and the treatments they are given such as pain relieving medication can only address symptoms, and are not curative. After six months, when any specific disease has been investigated and excluded, they are given a diagnosis of chronic fatigue syndrome. (The recent provisional National Institute for Clinical Excellence (NICE 2006) guidelines will suggest that it is diagnosed after four months.)

Definitions of CFS

There are a number of case definitions of CFS, such as that of the US Centre for Disease Control (Holmes, Kaplan, Gantz, Komaroff, Schonberger, Straus et al

1988), and the Oxford Group (Sharpe, Archard, Banatvala, Borysiewicz, Clare, David et al 1991), and the different groups have somewhat different diagnostic criteria. A review by Mulrow, Ramirez, Cornell and Allsup (2001) concluded that evidence to substantiate the existing case definitions was severely limited. There is therefore some uncertainty about the validity of the diagnostic criteria.

According to the Oxford Group's diagnostic criteria (Sharpe et al 1991), the person must fulfil the following to receive the diagnosis:

- Have a principal symptom of fatigue with definite onset and not lifelong
- The fatigue is severe, disabling and affects physical and mental functioning
- The fatigue has lasted for at least six months, during which it is present at least 50 per cent of the time
- Other symptoms may be included such as myalgia (muscle pain), mood disturbance, sleep irregularity

Suffering from the following conditions excludes a CFS diagnosis: established medical conditions known to produce chronic fatigue, schizophrenia, manic depressive illness, substance abuse, eating disorder, organic brain disease.

Patients can vary in severity from being bed bound, to having a wide range of disabling symptoms, to perhaps just having fatigue symptoms and moderate disability. Patients who are encountered in primary care settings are probably less likely to be severely affected than those who are seen in specialist services or general hospitals, and clinical experience suggests that they will be more easily helped.

The condition is controversial; the initial debates were around whether it was really an illness, or just an extreme version of tiredness. More recently it has been more accepted as an illness (Department of Health 2002). It was also debated whether it is a new condition or has always been around; a review of the historical evidence indicated that there are good records of similar conditions in the past, the most common diagnosis being neurasthenia (Demitrack and Abbey 1996). A more unresolved debate is the extent to which it is a 'physical' or 'psychological' condition, and there have been a number of CFS advocacy groups who argue for it to be seen as primarily a physical condition, and this has caused some tension with health care providers who may put more emphasis on psychological factors.

Patient example: Paul was a student at a local university. Around the times of exams he started feeling very tired; he had found his whole degree quite demanding. A few weeks into being tired he developed a virus with symptoms of high temperature, muscle aches, and general malaise. He was advised by his GP to rest and told that the symptoms would eventually clear up. After a month he still felt very tired, and he was unable to get rid of muscle aches, and a sense that his temperature was not quite right. After nine months when he was struggling to continue his university work he was fully investigated by a physician and no signs of infection or other physical abnormality were found. He was surprised to be given a diagnosis of CFS and it was suggested he may benefit from CBT.

Cognitive behavioural therapy

Cognitive behavioural therapy, which looks at the interaction between the environment, thoughts, feelings, behaviours and physical states (such as fatigue), and which will be described in more detail in Chapter 2, has a good track record in the understanding and treatment of a variety of disorders. There were early successes with depression, anxiety, phobias, panic, obsessive–compulsive disorder and eating disorders (Blackburn and Twaddle 1996). More recently the range of applications has widened to include emotional disorders in people with cancer (Moorey, Greer, Bliss and Law 1998), people who have chronic pain (Eimer and Freeman 1998), and also those who have somatic complaints unexplained by organic disease (Sharpe, Peveler and Mayou 1992). It was thought, therefore, that CBT could aid the understanding of CFS, and improve the health of sufferers (as it had with chronic pain sufferers), particularly given the lack of alternative approaches to the condition: clinicians and researchers in the late 1980s started to think about what was causing these CFS symptoms, and started to develop CBT treatments for CFS.

A CBT model of CFS

The CBT model of CFS that will be used in this book will be described below and it is based on: historical developments of the model from the 1980s onwards; the evidence base to support the model, which will be reviewed; and finally the clinical experience of the author and his colleagues. The model is based on the idea that the symptoms of CFS are influenced by *predisposing, precipitating* and *maintenance factors*, as described in Figure 1.1.

It may well be the case that some maintenance factors are more important in a particular patient, or in the same patient at different times, for example stress may be a big factor but iatrogenic factors are less significant, or vice versa. It is important therefore, at the assessment stage and throughout treatment, to be continually assessing and evaluating the significance of each factor.

Patient example: Jane presented to the joint psychiatry/immunology clinic in the general hospital. She described symptoms of tiredness, aches and pains, dizziness and irritable bowel syndrome. She had a history of postnatal depression eight years previously, and had been on anti-depressants since then. Two years before being seen, she developed a bacterial bowel infection whilst she was on holiday, and struggled to recover. She did not (or was unable to) allow herself time off from work or from looking after her two children and her husband. She had initial symptoms of tiredness and bloating/diarrhoea and these symptoms worsened. Pain and dizziness appeared in time. On assessment, she identified beliefs that she was 'lazy' and 'I should always put myself last'. This led to a pattern of self-neglect and sacrifice that was a significant maintenance factor, alongside poor sleep and further viral infections.

Background to the development of the model

The model used in this book has been developed from previous CBT models of CFS and owes a lot to them. It is supported by the evidence base for the predisposing, precipitating and maintenance factors, and it is partly based on clinical observations. The hitorical development will be described below, and will be of more interest to readers who wish to understand how the current understanding of CFS came about.

Historical development of the model

The models of CFS that clinicians developed differed somewhat between research centres, and there have also been developments over the years. In one of the first papers to describe a CBT approach to CFS (Wessely, David, Butler and Chalder 1989) it was suggested that the patient develops an 'acute illness probably infectious in origin'. There is then a reduction or avoidance of activity, a subsequent loss of tolerance, or reduction in fitness, so symptoms are developed at lower levels of activity. Patients' cognitions may include thoughts about making themselves worse if they carry on, and that there is something seriously wrong with them; and 'this leads to a vicious circle of increased avoidance, inactivity and fatigue' (Wessely et al 1989). Other points made in the paper are that it is important to acknowledge the person's distress, that patients should have psychological disorders treated, that therapeutic caution should be exercised if the patient is considering going on long term benefits, and that untested alternative treatments should be viewed cautiously. The main focus of treatment is exercise and activity, correcting cognitive distortions, limiting hospital visits, and the use of a co-therapist (i.e. a relative or friend to help with the programme).

Sharpe and Chalder (1994) built on the above work, and described a model that emphasises:

- Focussing on factors that are *perpetuating* (or *maintaining*) the symptoms: they argued that although *precipitating* factors like physical illness or stress may bring on the original symptoms, *perpetuating* factors lead to the development of chronicity
- Consideration of multiple *perpetuating* factors
- Identifying relevant factors by individual assessment
- Considering that factors may interact

This led the authors to emphasise a rehabilitative programme addressing anxiety and depression, physiological effects of inactivity, and cognitive distortions. In terms of managing activity there is emphasis on reducing the observed boom and bust pattern (sometimes called activity cycling), this being when patients do too much, feel very tired and sore, and then do too little. Emphasis is put on practising activities at a level that does not cause 'severe symptoms' and it is also important that the patient has 'planned rest'. It is also suggested that the clinician help with 'psychosocial problems', and also with sleep difficulties and hyperventilation.

The CBT approach to CFS was advanced by a group in Oxford, UK. It could be argued that their model of CFS (Surawy, Hackman, Hawton and Sharpe 1995) was more sophisticated, and a step forward from earlier work. There was an increased emphasis on cognitive factors such as:

- Negative thoughts about the effect of activity on performance
- The comparison of current performance with previous high standards, e.g. the patient believes that it is very bad that they are not able to do the things they used to
- Being over-concerned about the opinion of others

They identified typical personal rules (see Chapter 2) such as:

- A need to meet high standards and the unacceptability of failing to do this
- A need to be strong and not admit weakness

This model suggests that these rules/underlying assumptions are a *predisposing* factor to developing the condition; the authors accept previous ideas about *precipitating* and *maintenance* factors, in particular:

- *Precipitating* factors are a combination of acute illness and psychosocial stress. This may lead the person to press on and try harder to meet targets, until the predisposed person collapses in a state of exhaustion and frustration. The person may resist an explanation that they are failing to cope, and to save face prefer an explanation that they are suffering from a serious physical illness.
- *Maintenance* factors are an elaboration of the thought that they have a specific disease, and this may lead to avoidance of activities. Conversely they may episodically try to push on to meet demands.

Surawy and colleagues summarise their view as follows: 'a vicious cycle alternating between frustrated effort and ineffectual rest, maintained by the attributions of symptoms to disease, traps the patient in chronic illness'.

Figure 1.1 (overleaf) represents the model that is used in this book.

Figure 1.1 Cognitive behavioural therapy model of chronic fatigue syndrome.

Predisposing factors

Genetic factors (some evidence)

Possible developmental (early life) experiences that the patient had:

- Developmental emphasis on achievement/performance. (This could predispose the person to symptoms because it could encourage them to strive for performance in all or most areas at the expense of everything including health.) This could lead to the development of rules (see Chapter 2) 'I must do things perfectly', 'I must achieve'

- Emphasis on self-sacrifice (similarly the emphasis is on lifelong self-sacrifice at the expense of everything else). This could lead to the rule 'I should always put others first'

- Emphasis on emotional avoidance and control (there may be a long term tendency to avoid and control emotion, which could lead to emotional problems). This could lead to the rule 'I must always control my emotions'

Core beliefs (see Chapter 2) (could be predisposing or maintenance factor):

- 'I'm not good enough'

- 'I'm lazy'

(These beliefs could contribute to symptoms through the effect on the person's mood)

Precipitating factors

Physical illness (some evidence)
Glandular fever (some evidence)
Stressful events (some evidence)

Fatigue (and other symptoms like pain, frequent viruses, dizziness, and temperature problems)

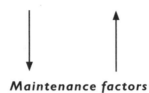

Maintenance factors

- *Emotional problems* (some evidence). As stated, problems with low mood, anxiety and other emotions could worsen the fatigue. These emotional problems may arise from life events, from the fatigue itself, or a combination of the two. The symptoms of CFS can cause problems with work, finances, family relationships and the ability to do basic tasks, which can be stressful. These emotional and psychiatric problems may be influenced by negative thinking processes as the CBT model would suggest

- *Psychiatric problems.* As was described above CFS patients have a higher rate of psychiatric disorder, that may be causing or contributing to the symptoms

- *Unhelpful responses to symptoms* such as overactivity beyond one's capability, resting excessively and 'boom and bust'. (Overactivity could worsen fatigue, resting excessively could cause deconditioning, and boom and bust could lead to poor management of one's energy reserves.) Again these patterns may be driven by particular rules, beliefs and thoughts such as 'I'm lazy', 'If I push on I'll make myself much worse', 'If you're fatigued, you should battle through', 'If you're fatigued you need to rest to get better', 'I don't want to burden anyone with my problems'

- *Poor sleep patterns* could worsen fatigue, although as described below the research evidence is unclear as to whether this is a major problem. Clinically it is observed that patients do frequently have sleep problems

- *Physical illness.* There are a number of physical illnesses in which fatigue is a common problem. The complexity arises when patients have a diagnosis of CFS and a particular physical illness. The issue for the clinician is to determine how much the other maintaining factors are significant, against the impact of this particular physical illness. If patients have both diagnoses, then there is often a suggestion from the referring physician, who made the physical diagnosis, that their symptoms are not entirely accounted for by this condition

- *Frequent viruses.* Many patients complain that they get a lot of viruses/infections that they have difficulty shaking off. These are likely to worsen their experience of fatigue

- *Iatrogenic issues* (this means problems caused by medical intervention). Sometimes medical advice is unhelpful. This may include advice to rest for an indeterminate period, to exercise excessively, to pursue excessive investigations. The advice, because it is not well targeted or precise enough, could be a maintenance factor. Alternative medicine may be helpful or unhelpful

- *Disadvantages in getting better.* Patients need to be supported when they are ill, but in a minority of patients these supporting systems can be a block to recovery. Disadvantages in recovering can be influenced by the dynamics of the family, the work and the benefits/insurance situation

What is the research evidence to support a CBT model of CFS?

Working through the idea of *predisposing, precipitating* and *maintenance* factors, there follows a review of the evidence around the CBT model: for CBT to be a meaningful approach it would be important to argue or demonstrate that maintenance factors such as deconditioning or stress or emotional problems are present in these patients and that there is a way in which they could cause or contribute to the symptoms.

Predisposing factors

Is there a genetic/familial factor?

Afari and Buchwald in their thorough review of CFS (2003) found that fatigue was moderately heritable. Chronic fatigue was more common in identical than non identical twins. They conclude that 'the family and twin data suggest that prolonged fatigue and chronic fatigue syndrome may be familial and that genetic effects could be important'. They do caution on methodological problems in the studies.

What are the personalities of patients who have CFS? Do they have problems in their personalities, or do they have unhelpful assumptions and beliefs?

The CBT literature would suggest that personality variables might predispose the individual to CFS: in CBT terms this is usually seen as patients having unhelpful and ingrained beliefs about themselves and the world and rules about how they should behave.

Johnson, DeLuca and Natelson (1996) compared patients with depression, multiple sclerosis (MS), CFS and controls and found that the depressed patients had the most personality disorder, followed equally by MS and CFS patients, who had low levels of personality disorders (personality disorder is a psychiatric term for patients who have complex and longstanding problems arising from personality factors).

Buckley, MacHale, Cavanagh, Sharpe, Deary and Lawrie (1999) found that on comparing CFS patients with non-depressed controls and patients with major depressive disorder, the latter had higher levels of personality dysfunction than CFS patients, who had higher levels than controls. The CFS group viewed themselves as being more neurotic and less extroverted when they were fatigued. It was suggested that these dysfunctions are an effect of the fatigue. So here it is unclear whether patients have personality factors that could contribute to the fatigue or whether the dysfunctions arise from it.

Wood and Wessely (1999) did not find any difference between the personalities of CFS patients and a rheumatoid arthritis control group. They found no difference on perfectionism, attitude to mental illness, defensiveness, social desirability or sensitivity to punishment. Social adjustment was worse in the CFS group. Christodoulou, DeLuca, Johnson, Lange, Gaudino and Natelson (1999) did not find differences in the personalities of MS and CFS patients. So here are another two studies that did not find any difference in personality between CFS and medical patients.

Henderson and Tannock (2004) found personality disorders in 39 per cent of CFS patients, 73 per cent of patients with depression and 4 per cent of controls. They concluded that 'high levels of personality disorder are present in CFS patients who attend a hospital clinic and this cannot be accounted for by co-morbid depression'. Magnusson, Nias and White (1996) found that, in a questionnaire study of healthy nurses, neuroticism and perfectionism were associated with physical and mental fatigue, possibly through the mechanism of the adoption of dysfunctional coping strategies. For example being perfectionistic may be tiring both through the mechanism of trying to do everything just right, taking too long to do things and worrying if they are not just right. These two studies therefore found an association between personality factors and fatigue. Also, White and Schwietzer (2000) did find higher levels of perfectionism, particularly in the 'doubts over actions' and 'concern about mistakes' subscales, in the CFS group compared to controls. So these studies suggest that there is some evidence of perfectionistic traits in CFS patients.

Blenkiron, Edwards and Lynch (1999) compared CFS patients to controls and in contrast to the above did not find that perfectionism correlated with fatigue. They found that CFS patients had lower expectations of others, and set lower standards.

Van Houdenhove, Onghena, Neerinkch and Hellin (1995) compared CFS patients to patients with organic conditions and to 'neurotics', and found the CFS group to be more 'action prone'. It may be that being 'action prone' leads to excessive activities and tiredness.

Poulis (1999) did not find higher levels of alexithymia in CFS patients compared to depressed and control patients. Alexithymia is the inability to describe and express emotion and has been implicated in psychosomatic disorders, which may have similarities to CFS. Johnson, Lange, Tiersky, DeLuca and Natelson (2001) found that both CFS and MS patients had higher levels of alexithymia and depressive attributional style. The CFS group scored badly on 'others/doctors locus of control', indicating that they did not have faith in the medical system. It is suggested that these personality variables are the effect of dealing with a chronic disabling illness marked by uncertainty. Personality variables may contribute to the symptoms by poor emotional regulation and the adoption of poor life skill strategies.

Fisher (2003) found that CFS patients were overprotected in childhood: this may lead 'to a belief pattern about avoiding activity' in adverse situations such as being fatigued.

Conclusions on predisposing factors

Is there a genetic/familial factor?

The literature does suggest that there is some genetic/familial influence.

What are the personalities of patients who have CFS? Do they have problems in their personalities or do they have unhelpful beliefs that cause them problems? If this is the case, are personality problems a predisposing factor?

The evidence seems to be broadly against CFS patients having personality disorders, and inconclusive or more negative as to whether they have perfectionist or alexithymic traits in their personalities. The latter finding is quite surprising in that the majority of patients seen clinically do seem to have perfectionist traits. The contradictory nature of the results may be because of weaknesses in the research, or because of weaknesses in diagnostic criteria, or because there are subgroups of CFS patients in some of whom these factors may be important and others not.

There is evidence from one study that CFS patients may have 'driven'-type rules (Van Houdenhove et al 1995), and this accords with clinical observation. Clinical examples of this would be rules such as 'I must achieve at all costs', 'If I'm not number one, I'm nowhere', 'I must get to the top'. These are different to perfectionist rules, and less commonly seen, and reflect a high value put on personal success and achievement, over everything else.

It is not known from the research whether patients have a greater amount of low self-esteem-type beliefs such as, 'I'm lazy', 'I'm not as good as others', 'I'm stupid', 'I'm a failure', than the general population. To the author's knowledge this has not been investigated. Clinical experience would suggest that a proportion of CFS patients have these beliefs.

Precipitating factors

Do patients have precipitating events at the onset of the CFS such as physical illness or stressful events, as the CBT model suggests?

White, Thomas and Amess (1995) found that patients were more likely to have a 'fatigue syndrome' after glandular fever than after a respiratory infection. Candy, Chalder, Cleare, Peakman, Skowera, Wessely, Weinman, Zuckerman and Hotopf (2003) followed up patients who had infectious mononucleosis (glandular fever) in primary care; this was because of the evidence of a link with CFS. They found that increased baseline immune activation was associated with fatigue at baseline and three months follow-up. Severity of symptoms and illness perceptions were found to predict fatigue three months later. At the six month point fatigue was predicted by illness perceptions and being female; at twelve months by being more disabled at baseline, and being female.

In a similar study, Cope, Mann, Pelosi and David (1996) looked at the issue of which patients in primary care, who had a viral illness, were more likely to have CFS six months later. They found that CFS cases were significantly more likely to have a past psychiatric history and a current psychiatric diagnosis. At the time of the viral illness presence of fatigue, 'psychological' attribution style and sick certification were also risk factors for CFS.

White, Thomas, Kangro-Hillar, Bruce-Jones, Amess, Crawford, Grover and Clare (2001) in a large study in primary care tried to identify the factors after the onset of glandular fever that lead to the development of either a mood disorder or a fatigue disorder. The factors that lead to a fatigue disorder were a positive monospot test and lower physical fitness at six months after onset; also at two months after onset cervical lymphadenopathy and bed rest were significant. Pre-morbid psychiatric history, an emotional personality score, and social adversity predicted mood disorders.

These studies, therefore, looked at people who became ill with an infection and found that a wide variety of psychological and social factors contributed to them developing fatigue problems, which is supportive of the model.

Masuda, Nakayama, Yamanaka, Koga and Tei (2002) found that patients who had CFS that had not started with an infection were more likely to have family and developmental problems and chronic stresses than infection-free patients. They were viewed to be more neurotic and introspective than patients who had suffered an infection.

One study (Hatcher and House 2003) suggested that patients with CFS were more likely to experience severe events and difficulties in the three months and one year prior to onset of their illness than population controls. In the three months prior to onset 19 of the 64 patients (30 per cent) experienced a 'dilemma' compared to none of the controls.

Conclusion on precipitating factors

There are clear methodological problems in looking at *precipitating* factors because researchers usually have to look at things retrospectively, investigating why some people who have infections develop ongoing fatigue problems and why others do not. Glandular fever is associated with developing a fatigue syndrome. Other factors identified with developing fatigue after viral illness are severity of symptoms at onset, 'abnormal illness perceptions', being female, past and present psychiatric symptoms, bed rest, poor physical fitness, cervical lymphadenopathy (abnormal lymph glands in the neck), positive monospot (antibody) test, and stressful life events. This provided some support for a CBT model in that bio-psychosocial factors such as stress and poor physical fitness are significant as precipitating factors.

Stress is currently understood as a process in which a triggering event occurs, and it has been suggested that problematic events are those that are important to the person, overloading, ambiguous, and uncontrollable. They are appraised in a way that is healthy or less healthy, and a physiological reaction occurs in association with an anxious emotion. The behavioural reaction can again be seen as helpful or less helpful. Other factors that may be protective against stress are male sex, rate of recovery, and social support (Ogden 2004).

Stress is implicated as a cause of ill health, through two mechanisms: the first is the physiological changes from the prolonged production of adrenaline and noradrenaline, and changes that occur include blood clot formation, increased blood pressure, increased heart rate, irregular heart beats, fat deposits, plaque formation and immunosuppression. These changes can increase the chances of heart disease, kidney disease, and infection. Stress is often associated with muscle aches and pains (e.g. Ohrbach 1996). Stress can also cause the prolonged production of cortisol that can result in decreased immune function and damage to neurons in the hippocampus. It may also affect the ability to eat normally, and exercise (Ogden 2004). The stress–physiological relationship may be causing the symptoms in CFS in a way that is not completely clear.

Maintaining factors

Does physical deconditioning play a role in the disorder?

As with much of the literature on CFS the evidence around deconditioning is inconclusive. Afari and Buchwald (2003), in a review paper, report that CFS patients do describe less activity than controls. Physiological measures of deconditioning have shown mixed results, some showing abnormalities others not. Patients often fail to reach their age predicted maximum heart rate; they perceive the level of effort and subsequent fatigue to be higher than controls, and this may be a perpetuating factor in that they overestimate how fatigued they are. There is some evidence that CFS patients cope with fatigue by resting or avoiding activity, and this could cause deconditioning. To the author's knowledge there is no research measuring whether patients take on too much or are overactive.

Are sleep factors important?

Regarding sleep, the same review reported that patients complain of more interrupted sleep and daytime napping, and more difficulty falling asleep, and this would be backed up by clinical observation. Polysomnography (measuring sleep) has not shown a consistently abnormal sleep pattern. However this test has shown that some patients have sleep apnoea, which is treatable. Some researchers believe that sleep disorders are under-diagnosed in this group, and clinicians should always differentiate fatigue from sleepiness. General observations would indicate that lack of sleep will lead to tiredness problems.

Do patients have appraisals of their symptoms that are abnormal and unhelpful?

Regarding the issue of appraisal, Afari and Buchwald (2003) conclude that the evidence would support that 'the ways in which CFS patients perceive themselves, label their symptoms, and appraise stressors may perpetuate or exacerbate their physical or psychosocial dysfunction'. This may be problematic in that the appraisals lead patients to be avoidant (leading to deconditioning) or over-focussed on physiological factors, which distracts attention from addressing lifestyle factors described here.

Do patients engage in behavioural changes like activity avoidance, overdoing or 'boom and bust' behaviour that contributes to their symptoms?

Avoidance could lead to deconditioning, which could worsen symptoms through the mechanism of loss of muscle tone and cardiovascular fitness. Modest activities are then seen as tiring and painful, and are avoided leading to further deconditioning. Observation would suggest that taking on too many tasks/overdoing it/not taking adequate rest will lead to tiredness. However to the author's knowledge there is no research available identifying whether patients are avoidant, overdoing it or in a boom and bust pattern.

Do patients have problems with emotions or psychiatric disorders, and if so does this contribute to the CFS?

It is known that CFS patients have a current (25 per cent) and lifetime (50–75 per cent) prevalence of depression, so this is clearly significant. Although depression is a common occurrence in CFS, Afari and Buchwald (2003) see many differences between CFS and depression; also 'depressive symptoms could proceed, or occur in response to CFS'. So it could be that some patients are depressed and misdiagnosed as CFS; it may be that an element of depression is contributing to fatigue symptoms, or the patient may have become depressed in response to fatigue symptoms, but the depression may then be worsening the fatigue.

Looking at anxiety disorders, panic disorder is present in 17–25 per cent of CFS patients, whilst generalised anxiety disorder is present in 2–30 per cent, again this seems significantly high. Clinical experience suggests that suffering these disorders is significantly fatiguing.

Looking at neuropsychological studies, 85 per cent of CFS patients will complain of problems with attention, concentration, and memory abilities. However, formal neuropsychological studies have been inconsistent in their results: the weight of the evidence suggests a modest impairment in information processing, working memory, and learning, though global intellectual abilities are normal.

Conclusions on maintenance factors

Do physical deconditioning and sleep problems play a role in the disorder?

Patients seem to be less active in response to CFS, and this may lead to deconditioning. Physiological measures of deconditioning have been inconclusive. Patients' complaints of poor sleep have not been supported by polysomnography.

Do they have appraisals of their symptoms that are abnormal and unhelpful?

This is likely to be the case, particularly if they have a mood disturbance.

Do they engage in behavioural changes like activity avoidance, overdoing or 'boom and bust' that contributes to their symptoms?

This does not seem to have been addressed in the research. Experience would suggest that some patients are avoidant of activity, usually because they fear that it will cause or worsen their symptoms, but not normally because they will 'damage themselves' or 'cause a setback'. The extent to which their beliefs about causing/worsening symptoms are unreasonable varies. Many patients do appear to engage in a boom or bust pattern.

Do they have problems with emotional disorders or problematic emotional states, and does this contribute to the CFS?

These patients do have a higher degree of anxiety/depression, as described earlier, that may perpetuate CFS although these mood states may be an effect of fatigue.

Overall conclusion on research evidence for the CBT model of CFS

There is evidence that patients may have personality traits that predispose them to fatigue, as the model would suggest, but the evidence is inconclusive. There are findings that patients have more stressful events prior to onset, and that psychological and social factors influence the likelihood of developing CFS/fatigue after a physical illness, which is in line with the model. There are significantly higher levels of anxiety and depression, and sleep complaints, which could contribute to the symptoms (or arise from them). Patients may misappraise their symptoms in an unhelpful way. Some of the other constructs in the model such as unhelpful responses to symptoms, the impact of frequent viruses and the disadvantages of getting better have not really been investigated.

Research on effectiveness of CBT with CFS

Lloyd, Hickie, Brockman, Hickie, Wilson, Dwyer and Wakefield (1993) conducted the first randomised controlled trial (RCT) that compared their CBT approach with immunological treatments together and separately. The CBT arm emphasised increased activity and exercise, on the basis that inactivity was problematic. They found that no treatment was superior to another or to control. The authors acknowledge that CBT may have performed better if compliance was monitored more closely and treatment was prolonged.

In Oxford, Sharpe, Hawton, Simkin, Surawy, Klimes, Peto, Warrell and Seagroatt (1996) conducted another RCT which showed that adding the Oxford treatment model of CBT to routine medical care led to a sustained reduction in functional impairment. Deale, Chalder, Marks and Wessely (1997) conducted an RCT and reported that functional impairment and fatigue improved more in patients who had CBT than those who had a relaxation control. Their treatment approach specifically consisted of 'planned consistent graded activity and rest', cognitive strategies, and relapse prevention advice.

There have now been a number of recent studies done using CBT with CFS, and Whiting, Bagnall, Snowden, Cornell, Mulrow and Ramirez (2001) reviewed these: they concluded that three RCTs out of four showed a 'positive overall effect of the intervention'. One study (Deale, Husain, Chalder and Wessely 2001) followed patients up at five years, and found that improvements were maintained for some outcomes (global improvement and proportion of patients completely recovered), but not others (physical functioning, fatigue, general health, symptoms, relapses or the proportion of patients that no longer met CFS criteria). Deale et al conclude that 'cognitive behavioural therapy can provide some lasting benefits but it is not a cure, some patients have difficulty making further improvements'.

McCrone, Ridsdale, Darbishire and Seed (2004) compared graded exercise to CBT for fatigue in primary care and found that they were equally helpful but CBT was 'easier to sell'. There was a low recovery rate for the group who met diagnostic criteria for CFS, as opposed to just fatigue. Huibers, Beurskens, van Schayck, Bazelmans, Metsemakers-Job, Knottnerus and Bleijenberg (2004) found that GPs were unable to effectively use CBT for the symptom of fatigue in primary care, so this was not an effective intervention. Severens, Prins, van der Wilt, van der Meer and Bleijenberg (2004) evaluated the cost effectiveness of CBT with CFS, and found the cost per QUALY (a measure of quality of life) to be high. They did describe some statistical uncertainty, and suggested that the true cost per QUALY would be clearer in the longer term.

Research on graded exercise

Manipulation of patient activity levels is always a part of CBT treatment, so the data from these studies provide further information about treatments, Whiting et al (2001) found that graded exercise was effective with CFS, and like CBT had a high validity factor. All three RCTs that were evaluated showed benefit from graded exercise compared to the control groups. No adverse effects of the intervention were noted but two studies did report withdrawals that may have been related to the (challenging) nature of the intervention. The average dropout rate for graded exercise was 18 per cent and for CBT 19 per cent. This was high compared to the dropout from pharmacological treatments of 11 per cent. High dropout may indicate that the treatment is unacceptable or has adverse effects.

Conclusion

There is evidence to support the use of CBT and graded exercise, but Whiting et al (2001) state that the research was often hampered by methodological problems, particularly the absence of standardised measures, little information on baseline functioning, different case definitions and exclusion/inclusion criteria. Many of the patients with the most severe symptoms were excluded.

Clinical experience

This author and his colleagues' own perspective on the patients they see is that they often have personality traits associated with self-sacrifice, perfectionism and emotional control. The patients have spent a long time acting in accordance with these traits, for example always trying to be 'perfect in everything'. A critical series of life events occurs, often a physical illness or a stressful life event, and thus the symptoms begin. The patients either rest excessively or are overactive, or alternate between the two. Treatment is usually activity management, stress management, and helping them to be less perfectionist and self-sacrificing. The outcome is usually moderate improvement in functioning/mood and mild to moderate improvement in symptoms. A number of patients do not really improve and a number are completely free of symptoms.

The approach in the rest of the book, therefore, will be to advocate the careful assessment of predisposing, precipitating and maintenance factors, and provide guidance on working with these factors, particularly maintenance ones. (It is possible to do a CBT approach that does not involve this kind of detailed assessment, so this would be an 'off the shelf' programme that provided a standard approach emphasising the things that are known to work from studies, primarily graded activity/exercise. There is no evidence as to whether this more protocol-driven approach works more or less effectively than a formulation one, but the latter allows for specific consideration of individual factors.)

Criticisms of the CBT approach

The CBT perspective on understanding CFS is not of course the only one. The other main perspective is that CFS is a physical illness, akin to diabetes or heart disease, in which the physiological pathology has not yet been found. This perspective would consider that any stress or depression that occurs in the condition is related to the effects of the illness on the patient and his family. The people who support this view are a (large) proportion of patients, and many of the CFS support groups like 'The ME association' (in the UK), and they would wish to see more basic physiological research, and more social support for patients who are disabled by the condition. They prefer to use the name 'myalgic encephalomyelitis' (ME), instead of CFS, or sometimes argue that ME is a different condition from CFS (Hyde 2003). There are frequent criticisms made of the CBT approach (see Gouldsmit 2003) and these criticisms include:

- The cognitive behavioural community overemphasises the importance of psychological factors at the expense of physiological ones. If this is true it may be because psychological therapists do not follow or cannot understand the complexities of biological literature (the reverse will also be true), and so this leads them to focus away from biological information. It also may be that because practically therapists can only work with psychological factors, and not biological ones, they tend to emphasise them unduly. Clinical experience suggests that the model of CFS that one would typically present to patients is sometimes less readily accepted than the models of panic or depression would be when they are presented to patients suffering from these disorders. It may be the case as the Oxford model suggests that patients resist this psychological model, finding biological explanations more comfortable, but many seem genuinely to feel that the CBT model does not entirely explain their symptoms. It may be the case that a more comprehensive CBT model can be developed that would be more acceptable to patients.
- The cognitive behavioural model does not pay much attention to strange symptoms like vertigo, nausea, intolerance to alcohol, intolerance to noise, visual disturbances and fainting that are seen in CFS. The model could only say that perpetuating factors such as emotional dysfunction/stress/ deconditioning caused these symptoms, and these are not symptoms that we would always associate with these 'stress' factors. This is a challenge to the CBT model.
- The CBT model implies that tiredness is on a continuum, yet patients will frequently say, 'this isn't normal tiredness; I wish it was. This is something different'. An answer may be to consider the situation with emotions; anxiety can be a healthy and functional response, but can become problematic in certain circumstances as fatigue can, and feels quite different from normal anxiety.
- Results from CBT trials often have a small treatment effect (Whiting et al 2001), which suggests that the treatment is inadequate to provide the significant improvement or cure that the patients wish for. This may be because of unrealistic patient expectations or inadequacies of the model.
- There is a considerable amount of research into the physiology of CFS, and this research is undervalued; although, in general, physical examination

and routine laboratory studies do not reveal any abnormalities. However, as Lapp (2000) says 'CFS does not fit the usual illness paradigm that disease is defined by injury, inflammation or malfunction.... CFS and related disorders have established a new paradigm: illness can operate at a deeper level where only specialised probing of the immune, endocrine and central nervous systems reveals evidence of malfunction and disease'. This has been done to some extent: for example, in terms of physiology one of the most studied areas is that of neuroendocrine function: according to Cleare (2003), there is on balance likely to be reduced hypothalamic pituitary adrenal axis (HPA) function in at least some patients (this refers to where the nervous system interacts with the endocrine system). This author is not competent to judge the value of this physiological research, but does fully accept its validity and importance.

• It is argued by some that the CBT approach drains funds and resources away from looking for the physiological abnormalities that will lead to effective physical treatments. Evidence for this would be that in the UK a large amount of recent funding has gone into a trial looking at behavioural treatments (PACE – Pacing, graded activity and cognitive behavioural therapy: a randomised evaluation). This would be a strong criticism if it were true.

Conclusion

There are criticisms of the CBT view of CFS of some validity. The view taken in this book is that there is a complex interaction between environmental, cognitive, emotional, behavioural and physiological factors. It is possible that intervening with any of these factors can bring about change. The CBT approach has a degree of evidence to support it but the effect sizes are not exceptional. It is important to pursue biological research and research into medical treatments: it may be that an optimal treatment is a combination of CBT and medical/drug treatment.

Chapter summary

Chronic fatigue syndrome is a disabling condition characterised by fatigue of at least six months onset, but which has not been lifelong, and which occurs 50 per cent of the time. There may be other symptoms. A CBT approach to this condition has been developed that attempts to understand how environmental, cognitive, behavioural, and emotional factors interact with physical symptoms. Some of these factors may be stressful events, psychiatric illness, unhelpful behavioural responses to symptoms, sleep problems, physical illness, repeated viruses, iatrogenic factors, and disadvantages of getting better. There is evidence that a CBT approach can help functioning and reduce symptoms. The evidence that supports a CBT model of the condition is inconclusive, and there are alternative ways of understanding the condition.

Chapter 2

Key elements of the cognitive behavioural approach

This chapter covers:

- What CBT is
- Padesky's five-areas model which considers the link between environment, thoughts, emotions, physical reactions and behaviours
- That thoughts can be problematic at different levels
- That the CBT style is active/directive and involves guided discovery and Socratic questioning
- That CBT structure includes agreement on length of therapy, agenda setting at the beginning of the session, homework tasks and the use of written materials like diaries and handouts

What is CBT?

Cognitive behavioural therapy is a highly structured, evidence based therapy that aims to address patients' current problems. The therapy is goal orientated, in that goals are agreed between the therapist and patient usually in terms of improving the patient's distressing emotional and (particularly with CFS) physical states, reducing negative thinking and unhelpful behavioural patterns. All of these may interfere with the patient's day to day functioning. Every aspect of therapy is clearly explained and the therapist and patient work together to solve the patient's current problems using a range of strategies, informed by a coherent treatment rationale, and working within an agreed time frame.

At a very basic level CBT looks at the relationship between environment, thoughts, feelings, physical reactions and behaviour (Greenberger and Padesky 1995). This relationship can occur at the levels of predisposing, precipitating and maintenance. This model is illustrated in Figure 2.1.

Five aspects of your life experiences

Cognition and emotion

Within the CBT model (Beck 1976) there are three levels of cognition (or thinking, content and process), the first being negative automatic thoughts. These are

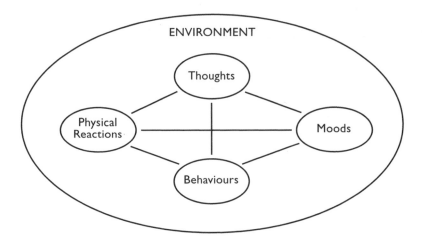

Figure 2.1   Five aspects of your life experiences (Greenberger and Padesky 1995).

an individual's appraisal of a specific situation or event or physical symptom. As such this level of cognition represents what is going through an individual's mind in a particular situation, and may be associated with functional, dysfunctional or neutral emotional states. Within the CBT model the thoughts that the clinician is most interested in are those associated with dysfunctional emotions such as anxiety, low mood, guilt, shame and anger. A dysfunctional emotion is one that blocks the person reaching their goals and/or is excessively distressing or prolonged. An example from a CFS patient would be 'It's impossible to do anything when you've got CFS'.

A further aspect of cognition at this level is the way in which the individual processes information, and Beck referred to this as thinking 'errors'. Research evidence exists (Clark and Steer 1996) to support the idea that in anxiety and depression the way information is processed is biased in a way that means only certain types of information are taken on board. For example in depression, not only is the content of thought negative but also information is usually processed in a black and white and over-general way. Similarly, when a person is anxious they tend to more readily pick up threat related information that maintains their perceptions that the world is in some way dangerous or threatening. It is therefore the case that patients with CFS who are experiencing these emotional states may misinterpret information. It is known that patients with CFS have more mood disturbances than in the general population (Abbey 1996), though how these interact with CFS is debated.

Patient example of thinking 'errors': Fiona was involved in a traffic accident in which she injured her leg. The medical evidence was that the injury had entirely cleared up, but she presented to psychological services with considerable pain and disability. Assessment indicated that she thought that if she walked then she would damage her leg further and this would mean it would be impossible to get back to work, with the implications that she would lose her livelihood. She also believed that if she walked significant distances the pain would be unbearable. She was in a dilemma about wanting to go back to work but being scared to do so. When she thought about this she felt extremely anxious and this led to excessive resting, avoidance of normal activities, and thinking about the pain and the threat to her job in a catastrophic manner. (This sort of scenario is extremely common and understandable.) A formulation and some behavioural changes helped her realise that her thinking about the consequences of exercise/activity was distorted, and that the anxious state she got into led to further problems. The behavioural changes were to gradually experiment with taking short walks and slowly increasing this.

The second level of cognition is rules (for living), also called assumptions. These tend to be applied across situations, so that they manifest themselves in several areas of the person's life. The behaviours that an individual does and does not engage in are useful markers for identifying the themes in rules. There are generally two types of rules. The first are those phrased as a conditional statement such as 'If I am not in control at all times then something bad will happen'. With this statement, provided that the demand of the rule is met, self-esteem remains intact and the person functions well. Onset of a disorder is often associated with a specific incident where the person's ability to meet the demand of the rule has been compromised, and they become depressed and/or anxious as a result. For example if a person has the rule 'I should never let people down' and they become ill and are unable to follow this rule then emotional distress may occur. If a person has a belief 'It is alright to be physically ill, but not mentally ill', they may deny any psychological aspect of their problems.

The other type of conditional rules are those phrased as 'demand' statements, such as 'I should be perfect'. These are often associated with a strong sense of duty and morality. A defining feature of these conditional rules is that they are held rigidly by the person, and it is this inflexibility that is ultimately problematic rather than the content of the rule itself.

The three broad themes in these rules are:

1   Perfection/high standards/doing things properly/living up to ideals, for example: 'If I can't do something properly there is no point in doing it at all'; 'If I don't always strive to do my best then I'm worthless'.

2   Approval/subjugation, for example: 'If I don't do what others want they will not like me'; 'If I put myself first I will be punished'.
3   Control, for example: 'If I'm not in control of my emotions it is a sign of weakness'.

The third level of cognition is beliefs, also known as core beliefs or schemas. These represent the mechanism by which information is processed by the individual; this is the engine that drives the psychological component of emotional disorders, of which conditional beliefs are a related process and automatic negative thoughts are a product. Unconditional beliefs are beliefs about self ('I am bad', 'I am a failure', 'I am weak'); self in relation to others ('I am not good enough'); other people ('People are not to be trusted', 'Other people are better than me') and the world ('The world is competitive', 'The world is not fair'). These are global in that they are held in all situations and have an absolute quality, in that people hold them as unquestionable truths. Thus, the individual finds it hard to distance themselves from the belief, but actually defines himself, others and the world by these beliefs. Thus, rather like the everyday givens we live by that grass is green or the sky is blue, these unconditional beliefs are formed in childhood and adolescence as a result of experiences in our lives. Whilst traumatic events such as abuse or bereavement and physical illness clearly lead to the development of very negative beliefs regarding self and others, most people's beliefs at this level are a product of their general environment during childhood, which will be a mixture of positive and negative experiences.

According to Beck's theory (Beck 1976; Beck, Rush, Shaw and Emery 1979), it is conditional and unconditional beliefs that represent the individual's psychological vulnerability to problems. Thus these beliefs may lie dormant but are activated by critical events that are related to them.

In the example above, Fiona's conditional beliefs are 'If I am in pain there must be something wrong with my body', and 'If I am in pain I should rest to allow my body to recover'. These beliefs arose from early experiences of her mother being physically ill and not coping very well, specifically by being very avoidant. Her core belief is 'I am vulnerable'.

From a theoretical perspective Beck (1976; Beck et al 1979) suggests that these thoughts give rise to unhealthy emotions and to emotional disorders. The emotions then function to keep the person focussed on the triggering situation, for example on physical symptoms, pain disability and their consequences. Behavioural patterns, often avoidance and withdrawal, or conversely overdoing it, then become unhelpful and contribute to the maintenance of the physical and emotional problems.

If distorted cognitions are identified in patients with physical symptoms then the overall aim of CBT is to modify each level of cognition. There is an assumption that work always starts at the level of negative automatic thoughts. This is based on the belief that this is the most readily accessible aspect of cognition and the one that can most readily be tackled, resulting in the most rapid symptom relief. A further reason for not tackling conditional and unconditional beliefs in the first instance is that these are more closely associated with core constructs of self; tackling these is likely to give rise to high levels of emotion. Thus, the individual needs to be equipped with skills to manage this emotion. These skills are derived from work carried out at the level of automatic thoughts. There is an assumption in CBT that each level of cognition is interconnected. As such, modifying negative automatic thoughts leads to increased flexibility in conditional beliefs and in turn direct work on conditional beliefs makes the processing mechanisms in unconditional beliefs more adaptive.

Cognitive behavioural therapy is therefore about identifying, understanding and breaking the vicious circle that is established between the person's cognition (negative automatic thoughts, rules and beliefs), moods, physical symptoms, behaviours and environment.

Environment

This can include a wide range of things: early experiences, past and current relationships; work and social milieu; past and present physical illnesses; stressful life events; etc.

Physical responses

The relationship between these factors and physiological responses was explored in detail in Chapter 1.

Behavioural responses

Unhelpful behavioural responses to physical and emotional problems can include: various types of withdrawal and avoidance; over-activity and under-activity; excessive reassurance seeking; physical monitoring of body such as taking one's pulse, poking, prodding, rubbing, and guarding areas of one's body.

Basic formulation of unexplained symptoms

In conditions such as CFS where there is no clear physical pathology, the CBT formulation would focus on how factors in the five areas of environment, cognition, emotion, mood, and behaviour would influence or even cause symptoms in the physical area. In developing any formulation in CBT, there would also be a consideration of how the five areas could be predisposing factors (such as genes, rules and beliefs), precipitating factors (including life events and physical illness), and maintenance factors (such as negative thinking, unhealthy emotional responses, sleep problems and so on).

Principles of CBT

The key principles of CBT are as follows (Blackburn and Twaddle 1996):

1   The importance of a shared understanding or formulation of the problem.
2   Emphasis on the patient's distinctive experience.
3   The collaborative nature of the therapeutic relationship (more recently the inter-personal dynamics between therapist and patient has been emphasised).
4   Active involvement of the patient, particularly in devising homework tasks.
5   The use of Socratic questioning (Padesky 1994). This essentially means asking the patient questions in such a way that a dialogue occurs that aids patient self-knowledge.
6   Explicitness of the therapist – usually little or nothing should be kept back from the patient.
7   Emphasis on empiricism, which means gaining knowledge from experience.
8   The importance placed upon what happens outside the session.

The main treatment strategies in CBT with CFS would include changing unhelpful thinking, problem solving, stress management, activity scheduling, pain and symptoms management, medication management and sleep improvement. These would have the aim of:

- Helping the person reach their goals
- Improving symptoms, functioning or disability
- Modifying cognition

Who will best respond to treatment?

An important consideration in deciding which patients will benefit most from treatment is the evidence base for CBT. The cognitive behavioural model has a long tradition of evaluating its efficacy and there is a robust set of research evidence demonstrating its utility in the treatment of a variety of psychological disorders and chronic physical illness (Department of Health 2001).

It is vital that cognitive behavioural interventions are not seen as a panacea for tackling all problems, and an important consideration is the goal of the intervention to be made, namely, is the goal to treat the individual so that they become largely symptom free or is it to help the individual to better manage a chronic and enduring illness? For many patients the latter is often a more realistic goal.

The CBT assessment process can be applied to any patient presentation; however the same is not necessarily true for CBT interventions. Decisions regarding which patients will benefit from a CBT intervention are complex and a number of factors play a role. These include: the nature of the presenting problem and its chronicity; the degree to which the patient accepts the CBT rationale; personality factors; hopelessness and pessimism. In addition factors such as the level of

clinician's training and skill in delivering the intervention, and the clinician's op-
timism/pessimism regarding the client, also exert significant impact on treatment
response. There is much research still to be done in order to increase further the
effectiveness of CBT interventions.

A central skill for the clinician is making a cognitive behavioural formulation
of the patient's problems, and this begins with the referral letter. The information
contained in the referral letter enables the clinician to think about what particular
questions need to be asked about the presenting problem (i.e. pain/fatigue). The
clinician then needs to consider whether the problem described may be directly
amenable to a CBT approach or whether it needs to be managed in a more generic
framework, possibly, but not necessarily or exclusively, informed by cognitive
behavioural principles. Even if a decision is taken not to implement CBT protocol
based treatment the structured approach of the cognitive behavioural assessment
and formulation will hopefully inform and enhance the patient's overall management.

Style and structure of CBT

Introduction

In this section the style of conducting CBT will be described, including the structured assessment, the active directive/problem solving style, Socratic questioning, the structure of therapy itself, agenda setting in the session, and the formal
'problem and goals' statement. The use of CBT materials such as handouts, diaries, measures and self-help materials will be described.

Structured assessment

Therapists must ensure that they remain structured in their work and this includes:

- A focus on the goals of the assessment session
- The creation of an agenda of topics to be addressed that is systematically
  worked through during the session
- The effective management of time during the session
- The systematic gathering of information pertinent to the patient's problems
  using the CBT model
- Clarity in the therapist and patient's mind about any work that needs to be
  done at home prior to any further assessment session

Clinical experience indicates that developing a structured assessment style enables the collection of detailed information quickly. It also conveys to the patient
that the clinician knows what they are doing and has an understanding of the

problems. This is vital for encouraging hope and optimism in the patient. Development of this style dictates that the clinician continually focuses the patient on discussion of a particular area, and actively takes steps to prevent the patient straying from the topic at hand.

There are a number of variations on conducting an assessment interview and the author will describe one that he has found helpful, in Chapter 3. To recap, the goal is to formulate the patient's problems, assess suitability, and develop a treatment plan if appropriate.

If the person were suitable for a CBT approach it is common practice to draw up a 'Problem and Goals' statement (also see Chapter 3).

Active directive/problem solving style

In CBT, perhaps more than any other therapy, the emphasis is on an active approach to problems. Issues are seen as problems to be worked with and there is constant movement towards behavioural and cognitive change and the achieving of the patient's goals. In practical terms the therapist will have in his mind: an awareness of the existing and evolving formulation; a confidence that goals are being moved towards; a confidence that the patient is learning about their problems and is learning self-help skills.

Behaviourally the therapist will be keeping to the agenda of the session, limiting discussions that are drifting too far off the patient's problems, and generally being prepared to sensitively interrupt the patient if the agenda is not being followed.

Guided discovery and Socratic questioning

Guided discovery is when the therapist and patient work together to see if there is a different way of viewing things (Wills and Sanders 1997). The preferred style of dialogue that aids guided discovery is Socratic questioning. This means asking questions in a structured way, and using what is called inductive reasoning (inductive reasoning is drawing general conclusions from specific facts or instances). The Socratic method is not about making the patient see the therapist's point of view, but as Padesky (1993) puts it 'to capture the excitement of true discovery'. Examples of good questions are: 'What is the evidence that this is true?', 'How does thinking like this make you feel and act?', 'How does this affect your physical problems?', 'How does this experience link in to how we understand your problems?', 'What could you have done differently?', etc. The therapist would want to teach the patient to use these questions himself in difficult situations, perhaps by asking 'What's the key question(s) you could ask yourself in X situation'.

Patient example of Socratic questioning: Pauline had very severe pain and a rash on her face. She had a demanding job.

Therapist: 'What's your job like?'

Pauline: 'It's pretty tough teaching these days with inspections and such like'

T: 'Given that it's tough, what effect does it have on you?'

P: 'Do you want me to say it's stressful? Everyone goes on about stress these days'

T: 'It sounds like you're a bit sceptical, which is fair enough. I suppose I was wondering whether there was a link between your facial pain and stress'

P: 'I've not noticed it but it is possible. Perhaps I've been looking for a physical cure which no one has been able to give me'

T: 'Is there any way we could find out if there was link?'

P: 'I could give it some thought'

T: 'That's a good idea. Can you think of a way to see if there's a specific link?'

P: 'I'm not sure'

T: 'What do you think about keeping a diary?'

Structure of the whole therapy

When one is taking the patient into treatment then it is useful to have a sense of how many sessions the person will need and to plan for this. Standard CBT is usually described as 8–15 sessions, and the patient could be given this estimate if the problem is relatively straightforward. With complex patients, therapy could take longer than this timescale. One can consider discharging a patient into follow-up when they are moving comfortably towards their goals, and there is a confidence that this will continue because the person is equipped with the necessary skills and attitudes.

Agenda setting

It is good practice to set the agenda for the individual session collaboratively with the patient. One would expect a typical session to involve:

*   General review since last meeting (including physical symptoms, functioning, mood and suicide risk if appropriate)
*   Review of homework
*   Setting of new homework

- Specific issues that therapist or patient wishes to discuss (e.g. life events, physical symptoms, progress of therapy, relationship issues, etc.)
- Review of session

Homework

A crucial element of CBT is agreement on and completion of homework assignments. Homework assignments may include: completing a negative thought diary or core belief workbook; reading self-help materials; conducting behavioural experiments; practising a new behavioural skill, such as meditation or assertiveness; and pain management or sleep management activities.

Padesky and Greenberger (1995) make the following suggestions to make homework successful:

- Make assignments small
- Ensure they are within the patient's skill level
- Ensure they are set collaboratively
- Agree a clear rationale for the task and write it down for yourself and the patient
- Begin it in the session
- Emphasise learning, not a particular outcome
- Ensure assignments are always reviewed

Materials

There are a variety of materials used in CBT to enhance the process:

- Tape recordings of sessions.
- Questionnaires. It is important to measure problems accurately using published and self-created measures. An important point is that it is probably better to have a few questionnaires that cover the main problem areas that one encounters, and that one is familiar and confident with, than to have lots of questionnaires in the drawer unused. In general patients are happy to do questionnaires.
- Handouts/self-help materials. It is important to be confident that the patient reads and understands these.
- Note keeping. One should encourage the patient to keep notes, and also encourage him to store his CBT notes in a folder that he brings to sessions. One should also make detailed notes oneself particularly at the assessment stage, possibly during the session, but certainly immediately afterwards.

If you need to know more about the basics of CBT then good introductory books would be those by Hawton et al (1989) and Wills and Sanders (1997).

Chapter summary

Cognitive behavioural therapy is an approach that collaboratively tackles 'here and now' problems. A structured approach through assessment and therapy allows for a full understanding of contributory factors for the patient's CFS. A strategy within session, and through homework assignments, is developed to treat these contributory factors and help the person move towards their agreed goals.

Chapter 3

Assessing patients with chronic fatigue syndrome

This chapter covers:

- How to solve engagement problems
- Beginning the assessment, the main problem areas, and predisposing, precipitating and maintenance factors
- Assessment documents

Engagement problems

Patients with CFS may be reluctant to engage in CBT. This is because their symptoms will present physically, and initially at least they will be expecting a physical treatment to be provided. There may be varying degrees of acceptance of the wider factors that could be contributing to their problems. They may have a somewhat black and white view that something is either physical or psychological, and in some ways this can be reinforced by the medical system, which directs people down one of these two routes. They may fear that giving up an entirely physical explanation for their symptoms has disadvantages in terms of possible treatment and illness status (Sanders 1996). The initial medical contact, often the GP, will have to broaden the horizon away from expecting a medical cure to looking at factors that are contributing to symptoms, and emphasising symptom control, rehabilitation and adjustment. It is obviously very important for any clinician to be explicit and sympathetic in demonstrating their belief in the reality of the symptoms. It is also crucial to reinforce any helpful strategies that the patient is already using. If the patient gets to a CBT service (which may be linked to the GP, or within a specialised pain or CFS service, or in a general hospital) then they may present in a variety of ways as described below.

Patient examples

Debbie came into the office and started talking about her problems. She had a long list of clearly disabling symptoms including generalised pain, dizziness, exhaustion, and poor concentration. She had been given some analgesia and advice about pacing, but her symptoms had not improved. She was tearful and looked depressed and demoralised: 'I feel like my life's passing me by. I've been ill for eighteen months and I'm struggling to look after myself, never mind my family. I've been on sick leave but my salary's running out. I'm really desperate for help, but I don't know whether you'll be able to do anything'.

Paul barged into the office and almost immediately started talking in an angry manner: 'I'm really pissed off about being told to come here, because I haven't got a mental problem. I'm really ill, and I just can't understand in this day and age why something more can't be done about this pain. I've got a scan next week (which I had to fight for), and I hope to God that something will be found on this, so they can get on with treating me'.

Both of these patients have severe symptoms and are clearly disabled by them. Debbie is demoralised, has financial problems because of the condition, and displays a mixture of desperation and doubt. Paul has an entirely physical view of the problem and a degree of anger about the symptoms, the system's inability to help, and his perception that others think his symptoms are all in his mind.

Clinical experience suggests that patients can have a variety of reactions when CBT is suggested for them, which can include being:

- Motivated
- Desperate
- Angry
- Sceptical
- Uncomprehending

Patients may present with several of these reactions at once. The patient who is *motivated* is usually open-minded, keen to get help, prepared to listen and try to understand the CBT approach, but may have a healthy scepticism about it. They will give their account well, complete diaries and questionnaires, and make a good attempt to follow CBT protocols. If these patients have perfectionistic traits then they may actually be too conscientious and almost put too much into the therapy.

The patient who is *desperate* has been round the system, and is likely to have a variety of problems (financial, work, family, etc.) arising from their CFS. They present as very strongly wanting some kind of 'help', and may or may not be engaged with a CBT approach. They are often demoralised, frustrated and possibly depressed. Engagement is about instilling some hope that a CBT approach can be helpful, empathising with the severity of the symptoms and their effect, and trying to bring about some immediately helpful change that the patient can benefit from. An issue that arises here is how upbeat one should be about CBT. If one is too pessimistic then it is difficult to engage the patient in treatment, and if one is too optimistic the patient may develop unrealistically high expectations that may not be fulfilled, leading to self-blame or possible over-dependence on the therapist. The approach that is recommended would be to quote outcome studies (e.g. Deale et al 2001), and state that these show fairly modest outcomes. One could say 'In my experience some patients do very well and are free or almost free of symptoms, the majority make varying degrees of progress, and some patients make no progress. Often coping strategies and mood improve better than physical symptoms. Improvement is usually greater if we can develop a clear understanding of the maintaining factors and we can work together to modify them': clinical experience would suggest that this statement best describes the outcomes that can be obtained in routine practice.

The patient who is *angry* can be challenging to deal with. He has often been to various services, and has not been satisfied. He may think that he is being blamed for his condition or his symptoms are not being taken seriously enough or are viewed as being all in his mind. He may be angry with himself, his family or the health system. He has often been told to come to CBT. He presents as angry, not a good listener, sceptical, afraid of being seen as 'mentally ill'. The strategies to use here are to observe his anger, to empathise with the frustrating nature of the symptoms, and to agree that services are not optimised to deal with CFS. One should ask him his feelings about being sent to CBT. When one has finished listening one could try to address his concerns. The points to make would be: CBT is a coping and rehabilitative strategy, it accepts and acknowledges the physical reality of the symptoms; it tries, unlike some medical specialities, to look holistically at the problems; it is not saying that the patients are mentally ill, but it is saying that emotional and other factors can influence pain and fatigue. One could say that cognitive behavioural therapists work with people who have problems with cancer and diabetes, to help them cope better. Generally doing all this is enough to get the patient to accept an assessment, and further relationship building work can be done.

The patient who is *sceptical* has a reasonable understanding of what CBT is but does not believe that trying to alter emotional states or behaviours will have an impact on symptoms. He may believe that mood states arise from the symptoms (and of course this may be correct), and he may comment 'If you had this you would be depressed'. His initial attitude is one of cynicism and possibly boredom. He may challenge the points that the clinician makes. One probably needs to work harder to make the patient see the potential benefit, and it may be helpful to describe successes with other patients, again without being unrealistically positive. It is important to describe an interactive model here, in which maintenance and physical factors interact with symptoms of pain and fatigue in a dynamic way. If the patient does not accept this, then it may not be worth offering them any CBT, and one should direct them to another approach (if there is one available).

The patient who is *uncomprehending* may not know anything about CBT and may not be clear why he has been sent to the service. He will seem bemused and uncertain about the referral. Here, before one does a formal assessment it may be wise to explain a bit about the approach and its potential to help CFS patients.

Obviously the first session is very important and the clinician must balance helping the patient see the value of the CBT approach, being sympathetic towards their distress, and assessing and formulating their problems in a way that a decision about the potential benefits of CBT can be made.

Structure and content of the CBT assessment

General assessment issues

The aim of this section of the book is to provide clinicians with a template for carrying out a cognitive behavioural assessment of the patients' problems. Hopefully, through the course of the assessment process it will be clearer which aspects of the patients' problems may be amenable to cognitive behavioural interventions. If it is clear following assessment that cognitive behavioural interventions are not going to be used then the clinician will still have gathered valuable and detailed information that can be used to develop an alternative treatment plan.

Therapists should ensure that they remain structured as this is an essential element of CBT. Structure includes:

- A focus on the goals of the assessment session
- The creation of an agenda of topics to be addressed that is systematically worked through during the session
- The effective management of time during the session
- The systematic gathering of information pertinent to the patient's problems using the CBT model
- Clarity in the therapist's and patient's mind about any work that needs to be done at home prior to any further assessment session

Questioning style

In the CBT assessment the clinician should begin by asking open questions and then moving to closed questions, to get the specific information that will aid the formulation. It is very useful, periodically, to summarise the patient's history as it is given to you.

Interview structure and process

There are a number of variations on conducting an assessment interview and we will present one here in detail that the author has found helpful. To recap, the goal is to formulate the patient's problems, assess suitability, and develop a treatment plan if appropriate.

The format described here is as follows:

1   Brief description of the main problem areas.
    (Sections 2–4 below will give us information about maintenance factors)
2   Description of potential maintenance factors.
3   Description of each maintenance factor using the five-aspects model (Padesky 1996), which refers to the interaction of environment, moods, thoughts, physical sensations and behaviours.
4   Formulation of a goal in terms of each of the maintenance factors
    (Sections 5–8 below will give us information about predisposing and precipitating factors)
5   Onset and history of the problem.
6   Prescription drugs, alcohol, illegal drugs, and caffeine.
7   Personal life history.
8   Mental state examination.
    (Sections 9–10 below give us information that aids our understanding of the problem and their suitability for CBT)
9   Formulation.
10 Explanation, suitability and consent.

Beginning the assessment

When the patient enters your office it is important to have a welcoming introduction. One could say 'Dr X has referred you to me. What I'd like to do today is spend 1–2 hours going over the main problems that you have, then trying to make some sense of the problems from a cognitive behavioural point of view, and then decide together whether this therapy has something to offer you. We may be able to do that today or I may ask you to come back on another occasion. Is that alright for today? Would you like to say or ask anything before we do the assessment?'

At this point one can try to address the concerns of the patient who is motivated, desperate, angry, sceptical or uncomprehending, as described above.

Finding out about the main problem areas

After the patient has said what they wanted, the clinician has addressed any immediate concerns, and the patient has agreed to the assessment, the first thing is to get a general description of the problem areas. This would normally be a description of physical symptoms. It can be interesting how the patient presents their problem: usually they will describe the most severe symptom first. Sometime they focus on stress. Sometimes they focus on disability issues like not being able to work. A typical opening problem description would be: 'I just feel shattered all the time, it's not normal tiredness, and now I've been told I've got ME (I'm really pleased to get a diagnosis at last). I get pain and tingling all over, particularly in my back, and I feel I've got the flu all the time'.

One should make a clear written record of the problem areas that might read: 'Problems: fatigue, feeling shattered, pain and tingling, flu-feeling'. One would then go into details about each physical symptom, and one could ask the following:

- Is it there all the time; if not, how frequently does the symptom occur? (F)
- Does it vary in intensity? (I)
- What triggers it off or worsens it? (T)
- How intense is it on a scale of 0–8, 0 being no symptoms and 8 being the worst symptoms possible

(The acronym FIT, standing for Frequency, Intensity, Triggers, may aid memory.)
   The type of physical symptoms that one could look for include:

- Fatigue/tiredness/exhaustion
- Pain
- Flu-like symptoms
- Cognitive symptoms such as poor concentration, word finding difficulties and memory problems
- Dizziness/faintness/fainting
- Intolerance to heat/cold/alcohol
- Irritable bowel symptoms such as diarrhoea/constipation/abdominal pain/ bloating

These are common ones, but there may be others. One can ask 'Have you told me about all your symptoms?' Conversely, if time is pressing, one may have to stop the patient going into too much detail. Often symptoms such as fainting or cognitive problems or pain are the hardest for the patient to deal with.

Maintenance factors

One would then go on to ask about factors that may be maintaining the problem. One could either go systematically through the potential maintenance factors described in Chapter 1, or go with what the patient is providing. The first one is easier for the less experienced interviewer.
   To recap, the potential maintaining factors are:

1   stressful events/emotional problems
2   psychiatric disorder
3   unhelpful responses to the symptoms of CFS
4   poor sleep
5   physical illness
6   frequent viruses
7   iatrogenic issues
8   disadvantages in getting better

Stressful events/emotional problems

One is looking at whether the patient has frequent stressful events or their response to stressful events is unhealthy and problematic in that it leads to an emotional response, usually anxiety, which is distressing, prolonged and blocking the person reaching their goal. As stated in Chapter 1 this response could be problematic because of the physiological impact or because of the way the person changes their behaviour. Clinical observation suggests that CFS sufferers have an excessive amount of stress in their life, and as stated earlier one study (Hatcher and House 2003) indicates that patients with CFS were more likely to experience severe events and difficulties in the three months and one year prior to onset of their illness than population controls. In the cognitive behavioural model the healthiness of the emotional response would be mediated by cognitive (beliefs, rules and thoughts, and processes such as memory and attention) and behavioural factors.

Regarding beliefs, rules and thoughts, in the model proposed these could either be precipitating factors or maintenance factors or both. For example, the person has the rule 'I must put 100 per cent into my work at all times', and their anxiety about doing this leads to an increase in workload and fatigue symptoms. It is possible to say that this was a belief that was a precipitating factor but not a maintaining factor if they were off work. If they were at work it would be possible to say that this rule was also a maintaining factor.

The person may therefore appraise and deal with stressful life events in a way that is likely to lead to fatigue and CFS. Another possibility is that the person has had an excessive number of stressful life events (bereavements, losses, physical illnesses), and the number of events is a problem more than the way they appraise them and deal with them, as can be seen in the examples below.

Patient examples

Peter had a major operation following a serious illness. He was a businessman and the time off work led to financial difficulties, and the risk of losing his home. This proved to be too much for his partner who left him during this period. Unfortunately his mother also died whilst he was in hospital. In general he did not cope in an unhelpful way but his natural coping resources were stretched by these events and the lack of support. He suffered eventually from moderate CFS.

In contrast Alexandra had an underlying assumption about always putting others first at all costs. Her brother became ill, and she sacrificed herself in looking after him in a way that led to complete exhaustion, and indeed an inability to look after her brother further.

In trying to assess this one would ask the person whether they were experiencing an emotional problem at the moment or whether it had been a factor in their problems. If there is uncertainty as to whether the emotion is unhealthy then it would be deemed unhealthy if it led to dysfunctional behavioural patterns and poor goal achievement.

Unhealthy emotional responses to life events

In the previous chapter we suggested that patients often had unhelpful rules around the themes of perfection, achievement and self-sacrifice. It is important therefore when considering the maintenance of the disorder to ask about the frequency of stressful life events and whether the patients have dysfunctional rules that are being activated in the face of these events. The sequence of events in Alexandra's case was a need to sacrifice herself for her brother, which caused some tiredness whilst she was doing it, and when she was unable to do it she felt guilty because she thought 'I'm letting him down. I should be able to help'. Seeing her brother suffer a serious illness compounded this emotional distress.

In terms of assessing unhealthy emotional responses, one would ask about the occurrence of critical or stressful events, and one would then ask about the cognition, emotion, behaviour and physiology.

Patients can have a full range of unhealthy emotional responses to current situations and these can include anxiety, depression, guilt, shame and anger. If one established that the patient has an unhealthy emotional response then it is important to see if it is related to physical symptoms. This may occur as follows: frequent unhealthy emotions may cause or worsen fatigue. One could try to find out if this is the case by asking 'Do you think your anxiety is causing or contributing to your symptoms'. (This is easier to make sense of with symptoms like fatigue but less so with symptoms like cold or alcohol intolerance.) Patients often answer that it is contributing to them but does not cause them. They often wish to emphasise that the fatigue leads to the mood disturbance. One can easily get into a 'chicken and egg' discussion. The CBT approach would be to simply see the mood disturbance as a maintenance factor and suggest that the symptoms could improve if the mood improved.

Unhelpful behavioural responses may be:

1 With anxiety: avoidance, escape, reassurance seeking, safety behaviours.
2 With depression: withdrawal, giving up pleasurable activities, suicidal ideation or attempts.
3 With guilt: concealment, atonement.
4 With shame: concealment.
5 With anger: attack.

In the CBT model these behavioural responses would be seen as maintaining the emotional response, by various mechanisms. For example when the mood is depressed the person, by withdrawing and giving up normal pleasurable activities, stops himself doing things that would naturally lift his mood up.

The most common emotional response that patients have is frustration, and this may represent a self-criticism about not meeting standards of achievement. Another issue is emotional suppression or avoidance, where patients do not describe any emotions or seem 'flat' or 'empty'. This is often called alexithymia (which means not having a word for emotion) and has been significantly implicated in psychosomatic disorder (Henderson and Tannock 2004), although as stated earlier there is no clear evidence of it being present in CFS (Poulis 1999).

The questions one could use to determine an unhealthy emotional response to the symptoms are, for example:

- 'How are your emotions?'
- 'Do you have a problem with your moods/emotions (frustration, depression, anxiety, anger, guilt etc)?'
- 'Are you able to express your emotions normally? Do you keep them under control?'

These questions should be followed up by supplementary questions as appropriate.

In terms of assessing unhealthy moods one could again use the FIT approach. One would be particularly interested in the relationship between emotional disturbance or stress and the worsening of symptoms. If the patient can clearly describe a direct relationship then this is helpful for our understanding ('I had a lot of stress at work and I could feel the pain worsen'). Sometimes the relationship is that of having a long period of stress and the worsening of symptoms, and this may or may not ease when the stress stops. Sometimes the patient cannot see any relationship, and in this case it may be useful for them to keep a diary to establish if there is a relationship or not. Again, the aim is to assess whether the symptoms themselves are a trigger for an unhealthy emotion or disorder, and this can be investigated by questioning or by the use of the same diary.

Psychiatric disorder

The person may even have a psychiatric disorder that interacts with their symptoms (or possibly is the cause of them). As described in the previous chapter, many patients with CFS have anxiety disorders and depression. These disorders could worsen the physical/psychological symptoms. However, Tiersky et al (2003) looked at the relationship between functioning, neuropsychology and mood in CFS and found that psychiatric disorder did not worsen physical functioning, though having a psychiatric disorder as well, unsurprisingly, did reduce emotional well being.

Responses to the symptoms of CFS

There are a number of ways that the behavioural response to symptoms may be unhelpful. This will be reviewed in some depth because of its importance. The behavioural response to physiological abnormalities, viruses, fatigue, pain and sleeplessness (the physical elements of the condition) will be considered.

There have been three patterns identified in CFS patients that are potentially unhelpful:

1   Doing too many activities in a way that they have difficulty in managing.
2   Reduction or avoidance of activity.
3   Boom and bust.

DOING TOO MANY ACTIVITIES IN A WAY THAT THEY HAVE DIFFICULTY IN MANAGING

This may be both a precipitating factor and a maintenance factor. The person may have a style of keeping busy, being self-sacrificing, being a perfectionist, and working too hard, not taking breaks. One can see that overdoing it in this way will lead to fatigue.

REDUCTION OR AVOIDANCE OF ACTIVITY

Conversely the person may be doing too little in the sense that they rest or sleep excessively, they avoid tasks, they gave up easily, they stop work or household or leisure activities, and they give up or do not engage in exercise. This is more likely to be a maintenance factor. The problem with this is that it can lead to deconditioning. It is known that deconditioning is associated with reduced volumes of oxygen in the body, reduced muscle metabolism and reduced muscle blood flow (Convertino 1997; Kroese 1977), and deconditioning in normal subjects has been associated with slower recovery rates. Therefore changes in muscle function described by CFS patients could be associated with reduced activity levels (Wagemaker 1999). It is known from using pedometers and accelerometers that CFS patients have activity levels that are 58–75 per cent of controls (Van der Werf, Prins, Vercoulen, van der Meer and Bleijenberg 2000; Vercoulen et al 1996; Bazelmans, Bleijenberg, van der Meer and Folgering 2001). However Bazelmans et al (2001) did not find differences in *fitness* levels between CFS patients and controls.

The cognitions associated with reduced activity are likely to be 'If I do this I will worsen my symptoms in a way I can't bear' or 'If I do this I will make myself worse or cause myself damage or injury'. (Clinical observation would suggest that the latter belief is less common.)

BOOM AND BUST (SOMETIMES CALLED ACTIVITY CYCLING)

This pattern has been observed clinically with CFS patients. What usually happens is that the person may feel a bit better in terms of the symptoms, so launches into doing a whole host of activities. They often go into a kind of 'overdrive' mode; they then have a worsening of their symptoms and often 'crash out' and have a prolonged period of rest. This is viewed to be an unhelpful pattern because the person is not making good use of their reserves of energy. As mentioned in Chapter 1, in the Oxford model (Sharpe et al 1996) a particular pattern is viewed to be important: that patients have driven and perfectionistic beliefs that lead them to act in a way that leads to fatigue. When they become fatigued they are unable to fulfil the requirements of the beliefs (such as always being busy) and may become emotionally distressed because of this inability. Because of the emotional distress they push on, leading to further fatigue. They oscillate, therefore, between fatigue and emotional distress. One does indeed see this pattern in clinical practice.

The questions to ask to determine these behavioural responses are:

- 'How do you deal with the fatigue/pain in terms of your actions?'
- 'Do you tend to do so much that you struggle to cope?'
- 'Do you tend to do too little?'
- 'Are you in a boom and bust pattern?'

It is quite useful to supplement your questions with an activity diary (see Appendix 3.3), because sometimes the answers to these questions do not give you the information that you require. Often one needs to trust the patient's judgement if they feel that they are engaged in an unhelpful pattern. Some patients have been overdoing it for a long time and this may be a precipitating factor, and currently because of their symptoms they are inactive. It may also be difficult to judge whether a person is deconditioned or not. Some clinicians use pedometers to measure the amount of activity that the patient engages in and then compare that to the norm. The average number of steps taken by a healthy person is around 4000–6000 (American College of Sports Medicine website, http://web.utk.edu/~cpah/FitnessFocus.pdf). These inexpensive devices allow one to quantify activity levels.

Poor sleep

If a patient is sleeping poorly then this will contribute to their fatigue (as described in more detail in Chapter 6). One can ask what time the patient goes to bed, time taken to fall asleep, any awakenings through the night and for what reason, time awakening in the morning, and quality of sleep. One could ask about poor sleep hygiene such as over- or under-activity impeding sleep, excessive use of caffeine and poor sleep environment (noise, light and distractions). One should also ask about daytime napping as this could be impeding night sleep. One should assess the factors that are keeping the patient awake or awakening them, such as pain or worry. One should assess the behaviours that the patient engages in, which may be unhelpful: lying in bed tossing and turning, clock watching, focussing on the time spent awake, and so on.

The rationale for enquiring into the above is that insomnia affects one-third of adults occasionally, and 8–12 per cent on a chronic basis (Ford and Kamerow 1989). People will typically complain of difficulty getting to sleep, waking frequently through the night, early morning waking, and that their sleep is unrefreshing. It is still somewhat unclear how much sleep people exactly need. The average amount taken is eight hours and this reduces with age (Herbert 1997). If total sleep deprivation occurs then hallucinations are possible, although there are no long term consequences (Herbert 1997). Another important issue is that most psychoactive substances will affect sleep either because of the direct effect of the drug or because of withdrawal effects (Benca, Obermeyer, Shelton, Droster and Kalin 2000). Poor sleep hygiene (daytime napping, coffee and alcohol before bedtime, and excessive noise, light, distractions and so on) can be the cause of sleep problems.

Physical illnesses

It is possible to be fatigued by a huge range of physical illnesses, such as heart disease, diabetes, multiple sclerosis, etc. Sometimes, however, patients have a physical diagnosis and they are sent for a CBT assessment because it is felt that their physical symptoms are not accounted for by the medical diagnosis. In this instance it is useful to talk to one's medical colleagues and to peruse the medical notes to try to make some sense of this. If one is referred a patient in whom one cannot identify any maintenance factors, then one should not be afraid to refer the patient back to the physician, reporting your doubts, and if appropriate suggesting that they are looked at again from a medical perspective. If the physicians are saying that there is no treatable organic disease then it may either be an unexplained or undetected physical condition or it may be that the patient has a severe somatisation disorder that the CBT clinician has great difficulty in making sense of.

Frequent viruses

It is possible that some patients do not manage repeated viruses in the best way. It is obviously quite debilitating and in general it is suggested that they should manage viruses in the way anyone else would: this may involve a consultation with their GP, the taking of palliative medication and time to rest and recover. If they are doing an activity increasing programme as part of therapy then it is suggested that this is paused. The problem arises if the virus is very prolonged. There may be a case to help the patient get moving again and start their normal activities around the virus (the normal cough/cold viruses). With patients who are prone to these it may be wise to give them advice about staying away from people who obviously are ill, but this advice will not save them from general airborne infection.

Clinical experience would suggest that patients with CFS suffer more frequent viruses that have a longer duration than usual. The research indicates that CFS patients appear to show a wide variety of immune system abnormalities (Antoni and Weiss 2003). One could ask patients how many viruses they have had in the last six or twelve months, and their duration. Patients usually have a good subjective sense of whether this is more than they would expect to have.

Iatrogenic effects

Sometimes these are a problem with CFS patients. The situation has improved over the years, however it is possible that there are still clinicians who adopt an 'I don't believe in it' attitude, and this potentially blocks the patient from getting the diagnosis and access to help that they need. Some GPs and health professionals may give out advice that is vague or unclear. Clinical experience suggests that there are some patients who, having been told to rest by their GP were still resting several years later. No doubt the GP did not intend this but the result was excessive inactivity and possible deconditioning. Similarly, medical professionals give out advice to exercise and to pace themselves without explaining what this exercise should be in terms of intensity, duration and timing, or what 'pacing' specifically means. If one thinks this is a problem one should ask about it.

Disadvantages of getting better

It is possible that some patients may be disadvantaged by getting better. This may be because their illness allows them to gain some sort of psychological benefit, a benefit from a national or private insurance system, a benefit in their work situation (usually being off sick), or a benefit in their relationship with their partner or family. It would not be the author's experience that the disadvantages of getting better are a common problem with CFS patients. It is sometimes the case, however, that as the condition evolves some of these benefits become more advantageous and contribute to the maintenance of symptoms. This may occur at a conscious or subconscious level. It is not common in clinical experience that patients deliberately and significantly exaggerate their symptoms, although some exaggeration can occasionally occur if there are strong reasons not to get better.

The kind of factors that would suggest there are disadvantages to getting better are:

* The symptoms do not seem as severe as the patient is saying
* A very attentive spouse or family
* A history of dependent traits
* Financial benefits that would make getting well very disadvantageous
* The patient's story is muddled, inconsistent or hard to understand

It can understandably be difficult to assess these factors directly and to do so requires tact. It may be useful to speak to significant others such as the partner, family and GP. It may be useful to get all case notes. With some patients it is possible to ask directly but tactfully about these issues.

For example:

- 'What would things be like if you didn't have your symptoms? Would there be any disadvantages in getting well?'
- 'Have you got a bit stuck with the symptoms? Why is that?'
- 'Have you heard the term "the sick role"? Does it apply to you at all?'
- 'Can your family be over-attentive? Can that cause problems?'
- 'Thinking about your personality, would you see yourself as dependent or independent? Could you say a bit more about that?'
- 'Does the benefit situation make it difficult to get back to work? Could you say a bit more about that?'

In asking these questions one may get a variety of responses: a response may be to deny that there is any benefit from the symptoms, and this may be persuasive or not. It is also possible to get a response that accepts this, and one can then include this acceptance of some benefit from the symptoms in one's formulation. It is also possible to get a very hostile response to this line of questioning, sometimes justifiably.

Predisposing and precipitating factors

Onset and history

After one assesses the maintenance factors then one would move on to asking about the onset of the problem with an emphasis on precipitating events. One could ask: When did the problem first start? Was there anything going on in your life at that time? Did you suffer any physical illnesses/viruses? Did you suffer any stressful events? One would then go on to trace the course of the disorder, looking at patterns of remission, improvement or deterioration, and link that in to life events. This might give further information about predisposing and precipitating factors.

Information about predisposing and precipitating factors from life history

We then move on to considering the person's 'life history'. A good way to ask about it is as follows:

- Medical, psychiatric, forensic history
- Personality
- Housing, finances, hobbies
- Parents and siblings
- Birth, family atmosphere, upbringing, relationship to current problems
- Education, work
- Relationships and sexuality, friends and family
- Religion or spirituality

When starting to ask about life history it is useful to explain to the person why you are doing it; one would hope that the person understood that the purpose of doing it is to understand them better and develop a formulation. Regarding the medical, psychiatric and forensic history the first question is usually 'Have you suffered from any significant medical disorders?' and then 'Have you suffered from any significant psychiatric problems (that we haven't already talked about)?' Finally it is worth asking 'Have you had any involvement with the police, the courts or the legal system?' This will (hopefully) pick up if the person has any forensic history, or if the person is involved in any litigation. Asking about personality may be omitted if this has been clearly gone through in detail before. We covered it when we asked earlier about the sequence of cognition, unhealthy emotion and physical symptom.

One can then ask about the person's living arrangements, financial situation and hobbies. This will help discover whether there are problems in this area. For example, patients with chronic fatigue could have problems with their accommodation, or ability to pursue their interests. It is then worth asking about parents and siblings in terms of names, ages, occupation, and physical and mental health status. Relationships with these family members could be explored. Whether the person had any difficulties at birth, any problems with development milestones and early family atmosphere should be asked about. Whether their early life has any link to their current problems should be asked.

The person's educational history including academic achievement and any particular problems such as bullying, truancy and absences should be enquired into. Their working history should be traced, and their career aspirations (if any) should be asked about. One should explore their history of relationships and marriages, and any problems that occurred. They should be asked about the name, age and employment of their current partner, and the names, ages and occupation of children and the patient's relationship with them should be explored. One should ask about whether they have any sexual problems, and it may be relevant to ask cautiously if they have suffered any traumatic sexual experiences in the past. Finally they can be asked if they are religious or spiritual. As stated we are looking for factors that may be predisposing them to CFS.

Of course this results in a very detailed life history being obtained, but if it is not done then there is a risk that some crucial piece of information could be missed. If for the reason of time it is not possible to do such a detailed life history then it is possible to do a limited assessment by asking more open questions, followed up by more detailed questions if necessary. One could ask 'Is there anything that it is important for me to know about… (then go through)… your medical history… your living arrangements… your upbringing… your education and employment… your current relationships?' If one had very little time then it may only be possible to ask the question 'Is there anything that it is important for me to know about your background history?', but be aware of our earlier comments about the dangers of this.

Psychiatric diagnosis and mental state examination

It is recommended that a brief mental state examination be conducted. This consists of an objective assessment of the person's current mental state with the goals of obtaining a psychiatric diagnosis, if there is one, and assessing risk (Sims 1993). Obviously some of the information obtained here may have been discussed earlier and it is not necessary to repeat questions. If the person reaches the diagnostic criteria for CFS or a psychiatric disorder then this should be discussed with them.

In conducting a mental state examination, the first thing to do is to observe the person's appearance, voice and demeanour. One needs then to collect further information regarding signs and symptoms that would support any diagnosis that would apply. Obviously if one, say, believed a person was suffering from a diagnosable depression then presumably some of the symptoms of depression such as sleeplessness, poor self-esteem and withdrawal would have been discussed at an earlier stage. If one then wishes to make a diagnosis of depression then it would be necessary to establish whether the other signs and symptoms required for the diagnosis are present. It is then advisable to do a brief run through of other mental disorders to establish whether the person could be suffering from something that has been missed. One could therefore ask about obsessive–compulsive disorder, panic attacks, phobias, generalised anxiety (worry), post-traumatic stress disorder, bulimia, anorexia nervosa, psychosis and plainly depression if this was not the presenting problem. It may be necessary to ask whether they have the particular symptom that would confirm the diagnosis. It is then important to do a risk assessment regarding harm to self, others or children, and this should be guided by local instructions, but also by CBT principles. (See Persons 1989, Chapter 10, for a full discussion.) Of course depending on the time available it may only be possible to do a very brief mental state examination, but risk assessment must never be missed.

Concluding the assessment

This would now leave one at the end of the assessment and it is good practice to ask 'Is there anything that we have not covered or anything that it is important for me to know?' This occasionally reveals important information. At this stage one is in possession of a considerable amount of information. One would hope that there is a process of making sense of the information going on as the conversation continues. If the interview has been conducted with a break then it will have given one the opportunity to do this. If not, it is wise to ask the patient to go to the waiting room (and possibly begin filling in questionnaires), to allow one time to think. In this time one wants to arrive at a formulation of their problem in terms of predisposing, precipitating and maintaining factors, and then consider whether the person would benefit from a CBT approach. It is important that the formulation is shared and agreed: the patient should feel that it is a credible explanation of their problems.

The Assessment and Formulation process can be aided by the use of measures and questionnaires and we will now turn to this issue.

Measures and questionnaires

It is very important to use self-monitoring tools to complete the assessment process (Hawton et al 1989). Their use at the beginning of treatment emphasises the therapy's self-help, collaborative nature, and it can give information about many aspects of problems. The patient should be provided with simple and clear diaries; there are many of these around or the therapist can design them. The data sought should be relevant to the problem and the patient should understand why and how to collect it. The typical questionnaires and diaries that would be used here are:

- Activity diary
- Sleep diary
- Questionnaires that measure fatigue, pain, mood, and other symptoms (e.g. Fatigue Scale: Chalder, Berelowitz, Pawlikowska, Watts et al 1993; Brief Pain Status questionnaire: Eimer and Freeman 1998; Beck Depression Inventory: Beck et al 1961)

In practical terms patients should be asked to complete questionnaires in the waiting room, rather than at home, to increase the likelihood of return. The way to fill them in should be explained briefly. Self-report measures should be completed at assessment, beginning, middle and end of treatment and at follow-ups. They should always be reviewed carefully with the patient after completion. These measures are also helpful in allowing research and audit to occur.

Problems in conducting the assessment

In general it is no harder to do a CBT based assessment of CFS than it is with any other condition. Problems can arise at the formulation stage of the assessment. Formulation in CBT is the attempt to link theory to practice, to make sense of presenting problems in terms of existing models of disorder. Sometimes it can be difficult to make sense of the patient's symptoms in terms of predisposing, precipitating and maintaining factors, and a much extended assessment is necessary. With most patients it is reasonably clear how the predisposing, precipitating and maintenance factors could cause exhaustion and pain, but with other patients it does not seem convincing that these factors could cause such severe symptoms or the factors themselves may be largely absent. If one cannot convincingly formulate the person's problems from a CBT perspective then this may indicate that physiological factors are the most significant factor, or that the patient may have an undiscovered physical pathology. In the latter case the patient should be referred back to the physician. A further complexity is to consider how the maintaining factors interact with one another. Examples might be behavioural avoidance, which stops learning, or inactivity, which makes sleep difficult.

If it is clear that the person does not have an underlying pathology, and one can develop a reasonable formulation, then one should feed back one's formulation to the patient. It is important to assess how much the patient is in agreement with the formulation and feels it is a reasonable explanation of their CFS. If they do not feel it is a reasonable explanation they are unlikely to engage in a CBT approach.

When feeding it back it is useful to describe the formulation under the headings:

- Predisposing
- Precipitating
- Maintaining

Patient example: Paula attended for assessment and presented as a thin woman of 27. She was pleasant in her manner from the beginning and I did not feel I had any particular work to do to engage her. I started by asking her about her main symptoms and she described headaches, pain, nausea, exhaustion and excess of sleeping. I got more details of these symptoms using the activity diary (Appendix 3.3) where I could. I first asked her if her symptoms came together or were separate. With the ones that were bundled together I asked what triggered them off and she answered that it was 'doing something (particularly seeing friends), walking too far, overdoing it and stress'. She stated that stress was the main factor that had brought her CFS on in the first place. I moved on to ask about maintenance factors and established that her sleep pattern was awry in that in the early days of her condition, which had lasted two years, she was sleeping for fifteen hours and now she was sleeping very poorly. She was under considerable stress from the fact that her symptoms had persisted and this had the effect of her having long periods off work. When she was at work she found it challenging. There was additional stress in that the police were investigating her boyfriend and this was ongoing. She tended to respond to these stresses by worrying excessively. In terms of underlying assumptions we identified 'I should always put those who are close to me first', 'I should always give 100 per cent particularly at work', and 'If I don't do things perfectly I'm lazy'. We considered these beliefs with their associated self-sacrificing, driven and perfectionistic behaviours to be both predisposing and maintaining factors.

In terms of how she responded to her symptoms she was in a classic 'boom and bust' pattern in that when she felt relatively well she would push on because 'I've lots to do', causing a 'crash' in which she was unable to pursue her normal activities for days. There was a sense of desperation and urgency to get better, which led her to push on too quickly. Her goals were to feel only 'normal fatigue', to sleep eight hours a night and be refreshed, and to attend work regularly and be able to perform at a reasonable level.

We moved on to trace the history and we were clear that the significant factors that had occurred three years ago were the beginning and continuation of the police enquiries, her working in a very demanding job in sales, and having a bout of 'glandular fever'.

When we looked at her life history the significant factor was being brought up in a family of high achieving perfectionists.

In conducting the mental state examination I considered that she would meet the diagnostic criteria for generalised anxiety disorder, but no other psychiatric disorder.

We therefore developed a formulation looking at how she was potentially predisposed to the condition by her family background and her personality structure. The precipitating factors were a busy job that she pushed herself very hard at, the police investigation, and glandular fever. The maintaining factors were ongoing stress (from different sources) and the way she managed it, boom and bust patterns, and poor sleep.

She found this tentative formulation, which we developed together, quite credible. She was motivated to work on her problems and we agreed a course of CBT, working initially on the maintaining factors and then on predisposing factors.

Formulation for Paula

Predisposing

Family of high achievers/pressure to perform:

- 'I should always put those close to me first' leading to excessive self-sacrifice traits
- 'I should always give 100 per cent particularly at work' leading to traits of driven-ness, poor delegation and taking on excessive tasks
- 'If I don't do things perfectly, I'm lazy' leading to traits of always trying to reach an unrealistic perfectionistic standard

Precipitating

Stress/demanding job/glandular fever: leading to fatigue/headaches/pain, etc.

Maintaining

Worry/ongoing stress/poor sleep/ 'boom and bust': leading back to fatigue/headaches/pain, etc.

Chapter summary

Patients may be reluctant to present to CBT services for assessment because they may see their problems as entirely physical, or they may think there are disadvantages to considering CBT. If they do come they may present as motivated, desperate, angry, sceptical, uncomprehending or some combination of these. It is important therefore to work hard to engage the individual. When the therapist does the assessment it is helpful to focus on the goals of the meeting, to agree a clear agenda with the patient, to manage time well and to gather information in such a way that allows for the understanding of the problem and the assessment of suitability. The structure of the assessment is usually to ask about the main problem normally described in terms of physical symptoms, and measurement should be made of these symptoms. The maintaining, predisposing and precipitating factors will then be assessed, followed by evaluation of mental state. A formulation is developed with the patient and their suitability for the CBT approach is discussed.

Supplementary assessment material

- *Assessment prompt sheet.* When initially conducting CBT type assessments it is wise to use a prompt sheet, in order that important parts of the assessment are not omitted. A prompt sheet is provided for the reader's use in Appendix 3.1.
- *Balance sheet* (Appendix 3.2). If one asks the patient to write their most tiring and least tiring occupations on a grid this can help with activity planning and pacing.
- *Activity diary: frequency, intensity and triggers of your physical symptoms* (Appendix 3.3). It is helpful to give all patients this sheet in order to get a picture over two weeks of what symptoms the patient has, how severe they are and whether they are related to any other factors.
- *Sleep diary* (Appendix 3.4). Again if the patient has a sleep problem, a diary filled in after the original interview is helpful.
- *Problem and goal rating sheet* (Appendix 3.5). The abbreviations on the form denote pre-treatment, post-treatment, one month follow-up, three month follow-up, six month follow-up, and one year follow-up. This form would usually be filled in at the first session of treatment. The normal way to write a problem statement is to describe the problem in a specific way and outline the elements of physical symptoms, thinking, emotion and behaviour that are problematic. A poor problem statement would be 'I've got a lot of pain'; a better one would be 'I have pain in my back for 4–6 hours every day usually in the evening and it prevents me looking after my children as well as I would like to'. A poor goal statement would be 'Try to have less pain'. The goal statement needs to be in the first person, specific and measurable.

A good one would be 'In six months time, I will have pain that is 40 per cent less intense and I will look after my children at a level I am happy with'.

The measurement of these problems in the 'Problem and Goals' statement could be done at entry into therapy, discharge into follow-up, one, three and six month follow-ups at one year follow-up.

- *Behavioural change sheet* (Appendix 3.6). This is so that both patient and clinician have a clear record of the immediate behavioural changes that the patient will make between sessions. This sheet is mainly used when patients come into treatment.

Chapter 4

Beginning therapy

This chapter contains:

- Treatment approaches to CFS; including the choice of whether to use *self-help*, *individual* or *group treatment*
- *Sequence of treatment*, how to address *urgent problems*, and how to deal with some key *maintenance factors*
- The key *maintenance factors* that are addressed at an early stage are unhelpful responses to symptoms
- Increasing activities and exercise

Self-help, individual and group treatment

There are a variety of self-help type resources available to aid patients with CFS, for example the well established book 'Coping with Chronic Fatigue' (Chalder 1995), and more recently 'Overcoming Chronic Fatigue' (Burgess and Chalder 2005). There are of course a variety of general self-help advice books on CFS, but these are the main CBT ones. Clinical experience suggests that self-help approaches are more effective with less disabled patients who are motivated to work on their own, and that they will work better if they are backed up by some clinician contact. Patients who are not too disabled, with whom one can identify the clear maintenance factors, and who are well motivated, are more likely to do well with this approach. It is possible to recommend this type of self-help book either after a GP/primary care assessment or a CBT assessment, provided that the clinician is sure that the patient is not suffering from a medical illness. The clinician should arrange review appointments at two, four and six monthly intervals, depending on the patient's presentation. This author would try to encourage the patient to use a self-help approach after he had done a formulation of the maintenance factors and considered that the patient would potentially benefit. One might say to the patient 'From what you tell me I believe that you could help yourself improve with a little help. I suggest that you use the following self-help material (suggest something), and that you come back and review it with me in three months' time. It is most important that you read the book carefully and that you do all the exercises contained in it. What do you think of that idea?' Dependent on the response the patient would be given the material or advised where to buy it, or if he was not interested the reasons would be explored. In further sessions progress and the need for further contact would be reviewed. If the clinician is unable to give the patient any follow-up of self-help, then it is helpful to stress the importance of following the programme, and being self-motivated.

Individual CBT may be preferable because it allows for detailed assessment, formulation and an individually delivered treatment plan and follow-up. However it is more resource heavy and it may not be practical in all settings.

Again, group treatment can follow a full CBT assessment or possibly just a brief screening. The danger of a brief screening is that the full complexities of the person's problems are unlikely to be understood. It is possible that CBT is somewhat diluted by being delivered in a group format. A potential group programme would be:

- Assessment of the patient in terms of their suitability, and their willingness to work with the model
- Introduction to the CBT model of CFS focussing on predisposing, precipitating and maintenance factors
- Patient self-assessment of their problems in terms of these factors
- Completion of problem and goal statements
- Module on 'Managing urgent problems'
- Module on 'Addressing maintenance factors' including unhealthy responses to CFS, stress and emotional problems, sleep problems, physical illness
- Module on 'Addressing predisposing and precipitating factors'
- Module on 'Dealing with any other issues/problems' such as pain, poor concentration, irritable bowel, lifestyle issues
- Module on 'Integrating CBT with other approaches'
- Module on 'Maintaining progress/relapse prevention'

The group treatment therefore follows the same format as the individual treatment described below. The modules may vary in length. In group treatment, as in individual treatment, emphasis is put on learning, self-help, homework assignments and maintaining structure. In group work one can also take advantage of the support and practical help that the participants give to one another in group CBT (Kinsella 2002). Also patients may have ideas to help one another that have not occurred to the clinician.

These are some advantages of group CBT, but there can be disadvantages. The particular problems that can occur are that: there is inadequate time to individually address the problems of each attendee; patients may spend excessive time describing the distress of their symptoms and although this is understandable and important, the therapist needs to balance this with more active treatment; there may be higher dropout; patients may have difficulty getting to the sessions at a particular time and location because of their symptoms, however it may be possible to use e-mail or phone links to overcome their difficulties.

In terms of the format of the group it will probably be between 10 and 15 sessions and these sessions should be spaced out between 2–4 weekly intervals in order to allow practising of changes. Ideally there should be follow-up to ensure progress is being maintained.

Family involvement

This is an issue that may come up at assessment and treatment. It is possible to gain helpful information about the patient from their family. It is worth considering whether a member of the family could take on the role of co-therapist (it is a different issue if the family itself needs support because of the patient's illness). A co-therapist is someone who could help the patient implement their CBT programme. If it is agreed with the patient that there is such a person, then their role would be to understand the formulation of the patient's problems and the agreed goals, and to help and encourage them to use the CBT programme, for example going over the behavioural change sheet with the patient once a week, going along with changes that the patient asks the family member to make (if they agree with them), and so on. A problem here is that often the patient has been shouldering the demands that are placed on the family unit, and CBT changes may encourage the person to ask others to share the load and may help the patient be more assertive. This may affect the family dynamic, and needs to be borne in mind.

Setting

The setting of treatment is important in that it is recommended that patients are treated in an environment that is easy to get to, and is easily accessible for people with disabilities. A building that does not have extremes of temperature or noise will be more comfortable. A building that has its own gym or exercise area would be attractive in that activities could be practised at the time of the session. It does not have to be a hospital or health facility.

Sequence of individual treatment of CFS

This section is on individual treatment. The sequence of treatment is engagement, assessment of the problems, measurement of the problems, formulation, and agreement on suitability. When this is agreed, then a 'problem and goals' statement is drawn up. It is suggested that the following is a reasonable sequence for individual treatment:

- Managing urgent problems (described in this chapter)
- Addressing maintenance factors (this chapter and Chapter 5)
- Addressing precipitating and predisposing factors (Chapter 6)
- Dealing with any other issues/problems (Chapter 7)
- Integrating CBT with other treatments (Chapter 9)
- Maintaining progress/relapse prevention (Chapter 7)

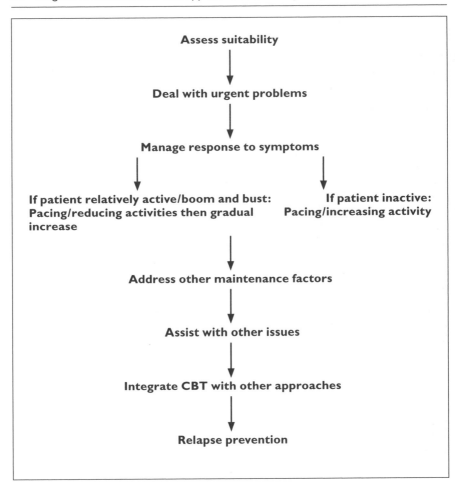

Figure 4.1 Individual therapy flowchart.

This is described in Figure 4.1.

Dealing with urgent problems

When one has completed the assessment, formulation, and 'problem and goal' statement, one has to make a decision as to how to start working with the patient. Often, but not always, there seem to be issues that appear very urgent, or are a 'crisis', and need to be addressed as a priority. They may be things that are causing the patient considerable distress, or will even interfere with their ability to co-operate with the therapy. Examples of these issues are:

1   *Very severe physical symptoms.* Patients may have problems with pain that may be relieved by analgesia, and if one has expert knowledge in this area, one could review this or advise consultation with their physician. Very basic distraction approaches can be suggested. Other problems that can seem urgent are fainting attacks, and when one is assured that this has been medically investigated then an applied tension technique can be tried; this is a muscle tensing exercise that has been used in blood injury phobia to reduce the likelihood of fainting (Ost and Sterner 1987). Concentration difficulties can cause problems as they make it difficult for the patient to make best use of CBT. Suggestions here are to limit the length of the session or to have a break during it, to tape the sessions, and to make ample use of self-help materials.

Clinical example: When Mr Wallace attended for his first meeting there was concern about the level of pain that he had. He had considerable difficulty attending to the interview. The strategy of the clinician was to help the patient control the pain but not be over-medicated. This patient was just on paracetamol that he took when the pain broke through. It was arranged to have this reviewed by a physician, as he had not been attending his GP because of their poor relationship. It was also advised that it would be wiser to take his medication on a regular basis.

---

2   *Ongoing stress/psychological problems.* Sometimes the person has an acutely stressful situation to deal with that is clearly causing or contributing to their CFS, and this may be a financial problem, a job issue, bereavement, a relationship problem, family illness, and so on. If the person has a situation such as this then helping with problem solving, helping the patient accept other support and then arranging this, practical advice or a helpful letter from the clinician may all be useful.

3   *Co-morbid physical illness.* Sometimes the patient may have a co-morbid physical illness like diabetes or rheumatoid arthritis that is contributing to their CFS symptoms. If the person's medical condition is responsible for their fatigue then that would exclude the CFS diagnosis. However, if it were contributing to their symptoms, but medical advice indicated that it was not solely responsible, then it would be important for the clinician or GP to ensure that this was being adequately treated.

4   *Urgent consequences of the effects of having CFS.* Here we would consider events in the patient's life that were very problematic at the time of assessment, and arise because of the impact of CFS. These could include a marriage crisis, possible loss of job, a benefits application, and so on. Again one would offer a problem solving/supportive approach here. If the problem is not easily solvable then it may be reasonable to encourage the patient to have a break from the problem.

Patient example: Hazel had been working as a nurse in the intensive care unit and finding it very stressful, and we agreed in formulation that this was one factor in the maintenance of the symptoms. When she first came to me she informed me that she was facing possible dismissal from her job because of impaired performance due to her symptoms. We both felt it was important to address this urgently, and we did so by discussing how she could handle the performance meeting with her manager, what her best interests were and whether a medical report would help. Attempts were made to negotiate with her manager around reducing the demands of her role, and a medical report was provided. The eventual outcome was that she was moved to a less demanding nursing role in outpatients.

5   *Sleep.* If the person's sleep were grossly abnormal then one would consider prioritising this through a medication or psychological approach, though the latter would be slower in having its effect.
6   *Complete inactivity/bed rest.* This poses practical problems in terms of attending sessions. It may be necessary to attend the patient at home, or possibly provide phone sessions. Someone with this degree of disability needs managing within the multidisciplinary team. A key cognition to work with fairly early may be, 'If I move/get up I will damage myself or cause pain that is unbearable'.
7   *Extreme over-activity.* Again one may encounter the patient who is so busy with the 101 demands they are trying to meet that they have no time to engage, and regularly miss sessions or do not follow the CBT programme. One needs to reiterate the formulation and treatment plan and work hard with the patient to reduce demands to such a degree that they will engage in therapy.

More details will be given later about managing the above issues. Some patients may not feel so 'urgent' and it may be possible to go more logically through the sequence of maintenance, precipitating/predisposing, other issues, integration and maintaining progress. What will be addressed next are problematic responses to symptoms, and this is normally the first maintenance factor to be addressed.

Addressing maintenance factors

Two problematic responses to the symptoms of CFS

If one considers that the sufferer from CFS has a wide range of very unpleasant symptoms that include pain, fatigue, dizziness, irritable bowel syndrome, concentration difficulties and rashes, then one can see that these symptoms in themselves are potentially very stressful, and difficult to deal with. The impact the symptoms have on the person's ability to live their life and the uncertainty about the future also have to be considered. However it is possible that some sufferers manage their symptoms better than others do. In the assessment phase one would evaluate how the person has responded to their symptoms. As described earlier one would look for a set of thoughts/beliefs causing an unhealthy emotional response, which will then lead to a particular unhelpful pattern of behaviour.

The emotional responses that are typically seen in CFS are anger at self or others (patients will often describe it as 'frustration'), depression, anxiety, and guilt. Looking at each of these individually, anger at self (or frustration) seems to be most common.

The two most common problematic responses to symptoms are:

1   Perfectionistic/achievement orientated thinking, leading to frustration linked into a behavioural pattern of either overactivity, or overactivity and then 'crashing out'. This type of patient would be characterised as the 'relatively active patient' (Bleijenberg et al 2003). This is possibly the most common presentation.

2   Thinking that is overpredictive of future bad outcomes, leading to anxiety and into a behavioural pattern of avoidance/reduced activity.

It is probably helpful to categorise the patient as one or the other. The formulation for Hazel, who was mentioned above, would be in the first category (Figure 4.2).

Managing unhealthy beliefs, emotions and behaviours in response to CFS symptoms

As described in Chapter 3 one would try to identify rules/beliefs, stressful events, negative thoughts, emotions, physiology, and how these lead to unhelpful patterns of behaviour in response to symptoms, and indeed in general. This would be written down and shared with the patient. At this stage one could then go straight on to simply getting the patient to alter the behaviour in the appropriate direction. (A more sophisticated way to do it would be to use verbal strategies to challenge the logic and usefulness of the belief, e.g. 'I should not rest until I have done all the housework, despite my symptoms', and then go on to identify ways in which a healthier belief could be more accepted, and this would involve cognitive, behavioural, interpersonal and emotional strategies.) It is normal practice at the beginning of therapy to help the patient to alter their behaviour as a way of making some progress around the relief of symptoms. It is therefore suggested that behavioural changes are made at an early stage in treatment, preferably after the assessment, formulation and problems and goals.

Helping patients with the two responses: the active patient and the inactive patient

As stated above one encounters two patterns of behaviour with the more perfectionistic and driven person, and these patterns are: frustration leading to a level

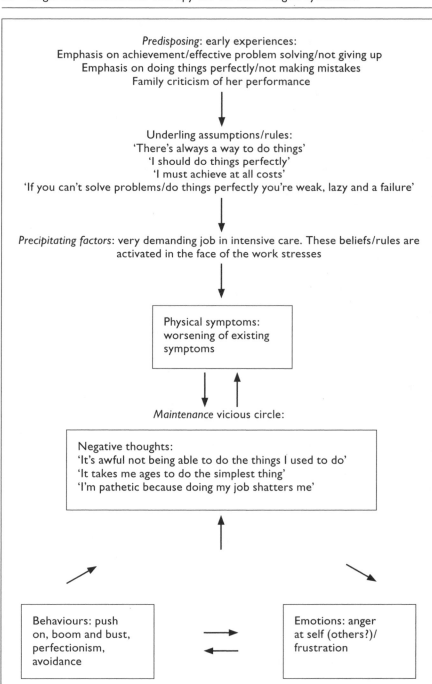

Predisposing: early experiences:
Emphasis on achievement/effective problem solving/not giving up
Emphasis on doing things perfectly/not making mistakes
Family criticism of her performance

Underling assumptions/rules:
'There's always a way to do things'
'I should do things perfectly'
'I must achieve at all costs'
'If you can't solve problems/do things perfectly you're weak, lazy and a failure'

Precipitating factors: very demanding job in intensive care. These beliefs/rules are
activated in the face of the work stresses

Physical symptoms:
worsening of existing
symptoms

Maintenance vicious circle:

Negative thoughts:
'It's awful not being able to do the things I used to do'
'It takes me ages to do the simplest thing'
'I'm pathetic because doing my job shatters me'

Behaviours: push
on, boom and bust,
perfectionism,
avoidance

Emotions: anger
at self (others?)/
frustration

Figure 4.2   The formulation for Hazel.

of activity that the person finds unmanageable; and boom and bust. The person who is anxious/avoidant is frightened of their symptoms, and engages in a lot of monitoring, avoidance and inactivity.

Relatively active/boom and bust

If one has assessed the patient and it is clear that the patient remains over-active in the face of severe symptoms, then one could categorise such a person as 'relatively active' or overactive CFS. The signs to look out for are: taking little rest; working long hours; taking lots of responsibilities; rushing around. Usually they get to a point where they are exhausted and crash out for a certain period At a psychological level the person is likely to be telling themselves 'I need to do things perfectly... get things done... others can't be trusted' and sometimes 'I want to stop, but if I stop I'll collapse'. The mechanism by which this pattern could be contributing to symptoms may be the stress that arises from trying to do a lot, or the physically tiring effect of doing more than they can manage and having inadequate rest.

As described earlier Surawy et al (1995) identify a particularly problematic 'Catch 22' situation that the patients get stuck in, and indeed in the Oxford model this is a key maintenance factor. The situation is when the patient who has perfectionistic/high achievement beliefs is affected by CFS symptoms and feels frustrated, and then their options are to:

1   Continue pushing on and 'achieving', which will potentially worsen symptoms because of the effort required, but on the other hand would not lead to a belief about being a failure and subsequent emotional problems.
2   Not continue to push on and achieve, which will potentially lead to unhealthy emotions, but will require less effort and is therefore less tiring.

One can see that at a behavioural level this could lead to a boom and bust/activity cycling pattern or a pushing on pattern, and Hazel tended to engage in this. One could suggest that the boom and bust pattern is unhelpful because it is not allowing natural recovery periods. One can see that the continued pushing on is unhelpful because there is inadequate rest. A useful metaphor to use here with the patient is 'Driving a car at 100 mph until it's breaking down, and then leaving it in the garage for weeks'.

The specific behavioural patterns that people get into are:

- Not taking rests during tasks
- Trying to always obtain a perfect result
- Continuing to try to perform at a level that they were at before they were ill, or when they were younger
- Working excessively long hours/not taking breaks/working weekends
- Not being good at delegating tasks
- Having a poor balance between work, rest, exercise and interests

Sometimes patients push on with these activities even though they have severe symptoms. They describe 'running on adrenaline'. If they were in a boom and bust pattern then these activities would stop and the person may 'crash out' and:

- Spend excessive time resting
- Spend excessive time in bed
- Completely disengage from activities
- Take time off work

These patterns are not entirely driven by unhealthy beliefs and emotions but are also a response to the demands of day to day living. Issues that were addressed with Hazel were fear of making mistakes in a pressured environment, the stress of being observed because of weak performance, and few hobbies and interests outside work. When she eventually moved to a less demanding environment we were able to make some progress with these in that she developed some hobbies and took some exercise.

Thinking about patients in general, the next thing to do if one has developed a formulation that views the patient as 'active' is to see whether this is the patient's perspective as well, in other words whether you have an agreed formulation. Sometimes patients say 'It's not that I want to do all these things, it's just that I have a busy life'. Indeed in looking at their lives one can see that they do have excessive demands in terms of work, children/elder care, and so on. It may indeed be that they are handling these excessive demands reasonably well; it is simply the weight of demands that is the problem.

The next stage is to discuss why demanding over-activity could be a maintenance factor for the symptoms, and one should draw this from the patient, using the Socratic questioning method. The topics one would expect to discuss would be that overdoing it could be tiring and could lead to exhaustion, and the stress of trying to do too much could also worsen the symptoms. It may be the case that it is not the doing of a lot of activities that is the problem, but the person being unable to cope with the level of activity that is being pursued. If they were in a boom and bust pattern then one would expect to talk about it not being a good way to manage the energy resources that they have.

The next stage is to try to agree behavioural changes to eliminate over-activity and boom and bust patterns. One would agree behavioural change statements and write these on a sheet. The normal procedure for agreeing behavioural changes is:

1   Agree on the rationale for the behavioural change. This may be to learn something, to get fitter, to lose weight, to counteract stress, to be less exhausted.
2   Write out the behavioural change statement in the first person, and spell out specifically what the person is to do and what the timescale is.
3   Anticipate any problems in carrying out the changes. The two most common ones would be that they activate the person's beliefs about being 'lazy' or a

'failure', or they activate concerns about housework or job tasks not being done, and these concerns may or may not be reasonable.

4   Try to address the problems by helping the patient challenge negative thoughts and beliefs, or talk through ways in which other people could help, or tasks could be delegated. Sometimes this cannot be done and the person has little scope for reducing over-activity.

Suggestions to reduce activity:

*   Delegate more tasks
*   Take all breaks at work
*   Finish work on time
*   Help patient with medical evidence that they should reduce demands of job
*   Create time for themselves
*   Draw on the support of others
*   Engage in a relaxing pursuit such as listening to music, reading, games, and meditation. Sometimes patients will physically do less but they are mentally very active, often worrying about things. Activities should therefore be engaging and absorbing. One should ask the patient 'Did you feel fully relaxed when you were following the relaxing pursuit', 'If not then why not?'

Specific suggestions to get rid of boom and bust:

*   Plan your week and stick to it
*   Identify areas where you could reduce the demands on yourself
*   Do not be tempted to take on extra activities even if you feel more rested
*   If you do overdo it, do not then 'crash out', but try to stick to the original programme of behaviour
*   Aim to be consistent in activities and rests over the day and over the week

The name for this type of behavioural work is *pacing*; the key principle is that the same level of tiring activities should be done each day and those tiring activities should be spaced out through the day. The rationale of doing this is to increase the individual's stamina and energy.

A model of pacing is the 'peak stop activity' (Bleijenberg et al 2003). The first stage of this is finding a base level, which is the total activities that the person can do without causing *extreme fatigue,* and these may include activities of daily living, hobbies, work, etc. One should design a programme with the patient so that there is a balance through the day and through the week between activities and resting. For example a patient may make breakfast then have a rest, take the children to school then relax listening to music, then do some housework, then take a rest, etc. through the day and week. The exact duration of the activity/rest cycle is a matter of discussion and trial and error. Very tiring/demanding activities should be divided up through the day if possible. The baseline needs to be flexible and have some room to manoeuvre. The first thing we did with Hazel was to try to reduce her activities to a level where the symptoms were more tolerable. We had identified a life pushing herself in a demanding job, worrying and filling her evenings with housework, done in a very perfectionistic way. Her behavioural targets were:

1   I will always ensure that I take my tea breaks at work.
2   I will negotiate with my manager that I look after the less ill patients.
3   I will ensure I finish work in time.
4   When I get home I will do a relaxing activity (reading, sewing) for 30 minutes.
5   I will go for a 30-minute walk four days a week, before tea.
6   In the evening I will only do housework for 30 minutes. I will ask my husband to do 30-minutes worth of housework.
7   I will do another relaxing activity in the evening.
8   At the weekend I will have a balance between rest, housework and exercise.

On paper this seemed to reduce the amount of tiring activities and redistribute them over the week. In practice it was not always easy to finish on time, and to only care for the less ill patients, despite attempting to problem solve this. It was helpful to always take tea breaks though she initially felt a bit guilty as some people did not take them. She managed to do a relaxing activity but complained that her mind was not rested as she wanted to 'get on with things'. The exercise went well though half an hour was a bit ambitious and was reduced to 20 minutes to start. Her husband did do the housework but not to the very high standard she demanded, and she was tempted to take over. She did not spend her weekends purely shopping and working but did try to ensure rest and a balance and this was helpful. We pushed on trying to help her achieve these targets. There was some relief of symptoms but it became clear that the demands of the job interacting with her personality style led her to the extreme fatigue we were trying to reduce, and it was necessary to change jobs and hours, allowing her to more easily follow the behavioural changes.

A complementary approach that can be used is for the patient to have a balance between activities of daily living (self-care), activities of development and enrichment (hobbies, interests), family activities, and (paid or domestic) employment activities (see Fennell 2003).

The important thing is to write out specific behavioural changes to help the person pace themselves over the day and over the week. In summary the key pacing principles in working with the over-active/boom and bust patient are:

•   Help them bring demanding activities down to a level in which their symptoms are not so extreme
•   Ensure that they have a balance of activities between activities of daily living, enrichment, family activities, and employment

- Ensure that they have regular periods of rest, i.e. mental and physical rest
- Ensure that they are not in a boom and bust pattern
- When the symptoms are stable gradually increase healthy activities

Problems in dealing with over-activity and boom and bust:

1   *It can be difficult to assess whether the person is in a boom and bust pattern.* One can use diaries, which may need to be done for a month, and one can use a pedometer, but the end result sometimes leaves one rather unclear. It is often the case that the person has been over-active but is slowing down, and this can give the impression that they are under-active. Good questions to ask here would be 'How do you respond behaviourally to the symptoms. Do you tend to push on? Do you tend to rest? Have you always been in this pattern?'

2   *It is difficult to know at what level to pitch the reduction in tiring activities.* Often, as stated, this is a matter of 'trial and error'. Sometimes patients have a significant reduction in symptoms when activities are reduced, but many patients do not. This may be because the 'damage has already been done' by years of demanding and tiring activity before you see them. For patients who do have a reduction in symptoms this would indicate that the pitch is correct. If the patient does not have any reduction in symptoms but you and the patient agree it is a sensible and manageable reduction, then you have probably pitched it at the right level, but it is necessary to wait and evaluate what happens.

3   *Deciding how long to sustain the pacing/reduction in activities.* Some models of CBT would suggest that once this stabilisation of symptoms occurs, then one should fairly quickly build up their activities again (Bleijenberg et al 2003). If, however, one views these patients as having beliefs that they should never rest and must always achieve, then there is a danger of the patient increasing too quickly. Also it may quite realistically take the patient some time to reduce demanding activities. Clinical experience would suggest that some patients do need a significant reduction in tiring and demanding activities. It is clear therefore that the decision as to when to increase activities again needs to be based on the formulation and the patient response. One does not want to get the patient to return to their over-active/demand driven selves, but to a healthier level of functioning. This is often not easy. It may be that patients need a significant period of reduction/pacing to get benefit.

4   *The patient who does not benefit from this approach.* Often patients do not change quickly with CFS and they should be warned that changes are more likely to occur over the longer period (months and years) rather than weeks. This can be a problem as the lack of feedback makes it unclear whether the right track is being followed.

5   *When reducing activities/pacing in the very active person leads to the re-activation of self-critical core beliefs and negative thoughts, such as 'I'm*

lazy', 'I'm not good enough'. When this occurs it is crucial to challenge them as described in Chapter 5.

6   *Whether patients who are reducing activities should be encouraged to exercise.* We know that there is evidence for the effectiveness of exercise in CFS (Snell, Van Ness, Stevens, Phippen and Dempsey 2003). However we are dealing with a group here who make excessive demands on themselves and are pushing themselves hard, and there can be wariness about encouraging patients who are very active anyway to do more. Patients in the published studies were not separated into (relatively) active and inactive patients, and it may be that the inactive group benefited more. However if this group is not encouraged to exercise they will be denied an evidence based therapeutic option. (Often the patient in this group will say 'I'm very busy. I'm exercising running after the kids'. It is important here to help the patient see that this does not really count as exercise. The clinician could help by explaining that exercise is defined as 'a specific programme conducted separately from normal activities for a set period and at a set level, and comprising warm up stretches and anaerobic or aerobic exercise'.) The research evidence would suggest that the patient who is setting boundaries on excessive activities is also beginning to follow a *graded* exercise programme, pitched initially at a low level (so it does not lead to severe symptoms) and then gradually increased through anaerobic to aerobic exercise if the patient can tolerate this progression. It is therefore important that all patients should be advised to do a graded exercise programme, and that this is carefully monitored. The NICE guidelines recommend that all patients who wish to return to normal activities should be offered this (NICE 2006).

Anxious inactivity in response to the symptoms of CFS

The alternative response to the symptoms of CFS may be inactivity, particularly in response to anxiety about the symptoms, particularly pain. The two likely thoughts that will make the person anxious and inactive are:

1   'The symptoms will get much worse'.
2   'If I am active I will cause myself some kind of damage'.

The former is the most common and may be accurate or inaccurate. In assessing the patient one gets a sense that the person is very anxious about the consequences of the symptoms. They will describe these thoughts, will feel different degrees of anxiety, and may indeed have significant physical symptoms of anxiety. They may also be attending to the threat and to the symptoms in an excessive way that worsens the symptoms. In the chronic pain literature 'catastrophising' is one of the most significant predictors of poor coping and adjustment. (Rosenstiel and Keefe 1983; Sullivan and D'Eon 1990). The behavioural pattern of the inactive may be:

- Spending long periods resting or in bed
- Avoiding walking
- Avoiding normal household tasks
- Not attending work
- Relying excessively on others, and so on

Once one has identified this pattern then there are various strategies available to work with it. Similarly for the patient who is over-active one needs to develop a baseline, but in the case of the inactive person the purpose of the baseline is to try to increase the person's activities in a gradual way, and the baseline here is one that allows the person to function at a reasonable level without severe symptoms. Increasing activity would have no value unless one also challenged the cognitive distortions that went along with it, and these will certainly come to the surface. These thoughts may include 'I can't stand this pain… I could damage myself for life… I'll fall over…'

The work here again is a type of *pacing* following the key principles that the person should do the same amount of activities each day, and not respond to symptoms. With these patients one can devise a programme as described above but the intention here will be to increase activity and exercise.

In developing a pacing programme it can be helpful to use the idea of a behavioural experiment. This is a behavioural change that helps the patient gather evidence around the truth of a hypothesis. There are two hypotheses that need to be tested and the patient is asked to do something to test them out. If the person believes that he will damage himself in some way, then an experiment can be conducted around this. This is likely to involve small increases in activity and one can try to evaluate whether the person has come to any harm. The patient could consider doing some kind of survey, asking friends whether harm would be likely following a small behavioural change, though this experiment of asking friends may not be practical. Before this the idea of 'hurt not equalling harm' (Eimer and Freeman 1998) can be discussed with them.

For the patient who believes that they will have a significant increase in symptoms then a prediction can be made about how much pain a behavioural increase will cause on a scale of 1–10, and the clinician can then evaluate whether this occurs. Here it is better to evaluate over several trials of the behaviour, as the person may get quite severe symptoms with their first attempt if they have been very inactive. If one is successful then it is an opportunity to get the patient to be more active.

The issues that could be discussed are:

- Increasing activities will counteract deconditioning. Deconditioning is a deterioration in physiological functioning as a result of inactivity, and this may be a factor in perpetuating the symptoms, but as stated earlier this is inconclusive (McCully 2003).
- Increasing activities can give the person a sense of control, and a greater

opportunity to pursue pleasurable and mastered tasks, thereby reducing unhealthy mood states.

- Increasing activities may lead to a less unhealthy focus on pain.

Patient example: It was clear that Kirsten was very anxious about activity. She had been spending long periods in bed, looked anxious, and identified thoughts such as 'If I'm more active I'll definitely get worse. I could damage myself. The pain will be unbearable'. She was anxious and avoidant. She predicted that her pain would be a ten out of ten. We spent a long time on the therapeutic relationship, the idea that 'hurt does not equal harm' and the concept of deconditioning. She started off spending short periods out of bed, then short periods (5–10 minutes) standing, then taking a few steps, then increasing her steps. After three months she is able to walk a few hundred yards with tolerable pain, and treatment is ongoing. She rates her pain at seven.

Exercise therapy for CFS

As described earlier there have been a number of studies examining the role of exercise in the treatment of CFS. If one is going to use this strategy as part of a CBT approach then there are various stages that one needs to go through (Snell et al 2003):

1   *Engagement and education.* In Snell et al's (2003) approach the emphasis is on less vigorous exercise such as jumping and stretching (anaerobic exercise), as opposed to more vigorous exercise such as walking and cycling that involves the body's use of oxygen (aerobic exercise). The need for restraint is also spelt out to counteract the patient's potential for overdoing it. The rationale given for exercise is that it is helpful to counteract the person's deconditioning in response to inactivity. The patient can be told that they may expect improvements in strength and flexibility, reduced pain, greater mental clarity, sense of accomplishment, improved quality of life, greater ability to complete activities of daily living, and learning to use exercise as a positive coping tool for CFS (Snell et al 2003).

2   *Exercise prescription and monitoring.* Ideally patients should be assessed and monitored in an exercise laboratory or possibly physiotherapy department, but this may be unrealistic for the typical clinical setting. In Snell et al's programme, patients are given two stages of exercise, stage one being 'stretching and strengthening' and stage two being 'stretching and resistance training'. The first stage involves developing functional strength and would include hand stretching, grasping objects and sitting and standing exercises. The second stage is focussed on increasing strength and flexibility, and the

chest press is typical of these exercises. (The chest press is stretching a band that has been placed around the chest.)

3   *Maintaining functional gains.* This involves evaluating the gains that the patient has made and ensuring that they will be able to use the skills gained in the future.

When should exercise therapy be used?

There is evidence from RCTs of the benefits of graded exercise. It would seem fairly clear that patients who are significantly inactive would benefit because of the effects of deconditioning. The patients who are in the more active group may be less likely to be deconditioned, and exercise may be less helpful. Obviously increasing activity as described above is a form of exercise; however the exercise used in the trials was often of a more vigorous (aerobic) nature.

It would seem reasonable, therefore, to encourage all patients to do a graded exercise programme, as we know that patients in the RCTs did not suffer adverse effects, although there was a degree of dropout (Whiting et al 2001). The important thing is the degree of grading, and as stated one would normally start patients with exercise that does not lead to significant or severe symptoms. Obviously what is significant or severe is quite subjective, and this author would use as a guide symptoms severe enough to discourage or stop the person doing further exercise. If the person was managing to tolerate exercise/activity then it could be slowly built up. It would obviously start at something quite gentle, usually stretching followed by walking/swimming/cycling, and it could then be increased, usually at 10–20 per cent increments. A complex issue is whether it should be left at anaerobic exercise, as Snell et al would suggest, or whether the person needs to do aerobic exercise to benefit. As mentioned several of the RCTs have used aerobic exercise: Fulcher and White (1997) used a 'graded aerobic exercise' programme and indeed compared it to flexibility exercises with relaxation. The aerobic exercise patients improved more on fatigue, functional capacity and fitness. Wearden, Morriss, Mullis, Strickland, Pearson, Appleby, Campbell and Morris (1998) also used graded aerobic exercise (cycling, swimming, and jogging), physiological functioning was measured in a laboratory, and the aerobic patients improved more than the controls. Clinical experience would suggest, however, that some patients, particularly in tertiary settings, find aerobic exercise difficult to do because of the aftermath of severe symptoms. This author's practice is to start patients off with gentle stretching and anaerobic exercise, and to build them up to a level that they can tolerate; because of the evidence we would aim for aerobic exercise. A useful resource in helping patients with exercise are gyms and health clubs, where exercise equipment is available, and programmes are supervised by staff who are trained in exercise planning.

The provisional NICE guidelines suggest that adults with mild/moderate CFS should be offered graded exercise leading to increases in duration, then increases in intensity up to aerobic level. The clinician should discuss the patient's goals with them and explain that it may take months or even years to make progress. The NICE guidelines suggest that patients should exercise (5–7 days a week) at a baseline, then increase by 20 per cent gradients to a duration of 30 minutes. 'When the duration of low intensity exercise has reached thirty minutes, the intensity of the exercise may then be increased from their current level gradually up to an aerobic heart rate zone as assessed individually by an appropriately trained professional' (NICE 2006).

Strategies to enhance compliance

There are a variety of approaches that will ensure that the exercise is completed (Vita and Owen 1995):

- *Help patients to set realistic goals.* As stated, this is the most important issue. A judgement has to be made around this with the patient so that they do not do too much or too little. A useful publication to assist this is 'Chronic Fatigue: Your Complete Exercise Guide' by Gordon (1993), although some of the advice would be challenging for the severely affected patient. A typical programme would be stretching exercises followed by walking/swimming/ cycling. It may be helpful to have short bouts several times a day rather than one long period of exercise. An initial target may therefore be: five minutes of stretching followed by ten minutes of walking at a gentle pace, twice daily.
- *Be specific in the advice you give.* Again it is not helpful to give a verbal suggestion about taking more exercise, but it is helpful to get the patient to write down 'Twice daily I will stretch using the advice in the exercise manual, and then I will walk for ten minutes at a gentle pace for one week and then review'.
- *Provide choice and variety.* Patients are more likely to do the activity if they chose it themselves. There should be an appropriate range of options available to them. The clinician or patient may need to do some research as to what is available locally. Possibilities are walking, swimming or running. If patients can attend the gym then their programme can be supervised by a qualified exercise specialist.
- *Encourage patient initiatives and independence.* If the clinician and the patient have developed some good principles as to how they should pace themselves, then the patient should be encouraged to show initiative in developing their exercise regime.
- *Help the patient to focus on the value of the exercise.* Discourage them from seeing it as a dull activity.
- *Consider the appropriateness and convenience of exercise settings.* For example it is quite easy to do a walk, but swimming requires a lot of (potentially tiring) organisation.

Problems with instigating exercise therapies

1   The most common problem is that the patient has severe symptoms of pain and sometimes fatigue after the exercise. Patients will often say 'I did it but I was shattered' or 'I had terrible pains in the legs after doing the exercise'. In this circumstance it is best to make a judgement based on whether the pain is 'severe' and likely to discourage them from continuing the exercise. If this is the case it is probably pitched at too high a level, and could be reduced in frequency or intensity. If it is not severe it is probably better to encourage the patient to push on. The rationale for this would be: 'It is likely that commencing exercise will cause some pain and discomfort if you have not done it for a while. However there are significant benefits in continuing. It may help to energise you, it may lift your spirits and it should help with the unfitness that has occurred through inactivity' (if the patient has been inactive).

2   It is often very difficult to decide at what level the exercise should be. In certain settings, particularly academic ones, it is possible to measure physiological response, but this is not always feasible in routine practice. Obviously discussion needs to be had with the patient as to what they could reasonably do, and if there is any doubt it should be pitched at a low level and reviewed. Again if one wishes to get the patient on to aerobic exercise then the question arises as to how the patient knows when they have achieved aerobic exercise. The simplest way to do this is for the patient to measure their own heart rate by taking their pulse. Gordon (1993), having reviewed the evidence, suggests that the three factors of frequency, intensity and time are considered when planning programmes. Regarding intensity he suggests that CFS patients should aim to raise their heart rate to between 60 and 75 per cent of their 'maximal heart rate'. The formula to estimate the 'maximal heart rate' is:

For all women and sedentary men:
220 minus your age in years.

For conditioned men:
205 minus one half of your age in years.

For example if you were a 45 year old sedentary man your maximal heart rate would be 220 minus 45 = 175.

a   If you are minimally or moderately impaired by CFS, use the formula in the box above

b   If you are severely impaired by CFS, multiply your value by 0.95 to get your maximum heart rate

c   If you are debilitated by CFS, multiply your value by 0.90

So the figure of 175 for the severely impaired would be multiplied by 0.95 to reach 166.25. Once the person calculates their maximum heart rate, the person should raise their pulse between 60 and 75 per cent (not above 85 per cent), i.e. 99–124 beats per minute.

It is important to note that this programme is applicable to patients who are using an aerobic programme and even then it would be built up to.

3   Some patients, particularly those who push themselves hard, have difficulty sticking to the agreed exercise limits. They may agree a reasonable programme in the clinic but frequently exceed it. This may be acceptable, but may cause problems if the person then gets very severe symptoms that discourage them from doing further exercise, or they exhaust themselves from doing too much. In this case if it is thought that the patient may do this it is important that one asks them to try to stick to the agreed programme.

Chapter summary

When considering beginning treatment there are advantages and disadvantages of self-help, individual and group CBT approaches to CFS. It is also important to pick a setting that is comfortable and accessible. It may be necessary to initially address urgent problems like a job issue. It is then suggested that the person is helped to manage symptoms optimally: if the person is active and pushing on, or in a boom and bust pattern, then emphasis is put on pacing. Later on healthy activities can be increased. If the person is anxiously avoidant the emphasis is on pacing with a stabilisation of activities, and then an increase in activities and exercise to counteract deconditioning. The evidence base would also support using graded exercise in a careful way, starting off gently and building up to aerobic exercise.

Chapter 5

Helping patients with emotional problems

This chapter contains:

- The patient's emotional response to life events, as a maintenance factor
- The role of thoughts, rules and beliefs in affecting this response

Responses to stressful life events

The patient who has CFS may have a variety of stressful life events to contend with. If the person has self-critical beliefs or unhelpful assumptions about perfection, achievement, emotional inhibition and self-sacrifice, then they may not deal with stressful events in the best way. This can be a maintenance factor for symptoms and also a predisposing factor, as described earlier. If the patient has these beliefs then the following events could be difficult to deal with:

- Doing things in a 'perfect' way, for example because of increased job or family or educational demands
- Significant failure in one or more areas that thwarts achievement
- Very emotional circumstances such as a trauma, bereavement or relationship difficulty
- Either a situation where the person is unable to be self-sacrificing or, more likely, where there is a significant call to be self-sacrificing

The person may strive to fulfil these demands or give up doing so, with various stressful consequences. Often if the person cannot fulfil these demands, a self-critical belief becomes prominent. For example 'I'm not able to work at my job as a computer programmer, I must be completely useless'. This can then lead to a stream of negative thoughts such as 'If I'm useless my wife will get fed up with me, and leave me and take the kids', and the consequences of this are low mood and depressive behaviours such as withdrawal, which can perpetuate the problems.

An important strategy here would be to get the person to identify and challenge negative thinking at the level of thoughts, rules/dysfunctional assumptions and beliefs. This is a large subject and in the space available here it is only possible to give a fairly brief account of how this is done. It is described further in basic CBT texts.

Working with negative thoughts

The first stage is to educate the person about the link between negative thinking and what can be termed unhealthy emotions, and fatigue symptoms, and seek their consent for working in this area. (An unhealthy emotion is one that is prolonged, and blocking the person reaching his goals.) The next stage would be to get the person to become more aware of their emotions by getting them to keep a diary. This should be done if the patient is unaware of their emotions, is unable to label them, or is unable to differentiate them from their thoughts. One could ask the patient to write down every time they have an unhealthy emotion, and they should be asked to label it, and also to rate it on a scale of 0–100 per cent: this can help the person to gauge the intensity of the emotions. A standard negative thought diary can be used for this, and one is provided in Appendix 5.1.

Identifying negative thoughts

As described in earlier sections we want to link negative thoughts with unhealthy emotions. We therefore want to help the person identify negative thoughts (and indeed rules and beliefs) and help them see how they lead to unhealthy emotions and behaviour. Once one is confident that the person is more aware of emotions, then these are some of the questions the person can ask themselves to identify the thought:

- 'What was going through my mind that led me to feel anxious?' (Or whatever the emotion was.)
- 'What was I thinking about that led me to feel anxious?'

It may be helpful, particularly where the emotion is anxiety, to ask:

- 'Did I have an image going through my mind that made me anxious?'

Asking the question in this way helps to reinforce the part of the model that says that it is mainly their thinking that leads to the emotion.

Using the negative thought diary

It is important when introducing the patient to the negative thought diary to consider:

1   At what point in the therapy this should be done.

2   How best to help the patient understand the rationale for using the diary.
3   How to deal with the person's concerns about the diary.

Regarding the issue of when the diary should be introduced it is suggested that this be done at an early stage. It is suggested that the following strategy is used to help the person consider using the negative thought technique. The clinician needs to remind the patient of the key elements of the therapy, and the clinician would then say something like 'Would you like to learn a helpful approach to working with negative thoughts?' One would discuss with them about negative thinking leading to emotional and behavioural problems that could be contributing to their symptoms. When the clinician receives the patient's consent she would reiterate the CBT model using an example that sums it up and links in to the diary process. For example she would ask: 'Imagine a situation where a manager comes in and gives some criticism to one of his employees, who has had a lot of sick time...' (it is best here not to personalise it by asking the patient how they would react themselves). 'How would that person feel in that situation...?' (Hopefully the patient would be able to describe an emotional state and one would be looking for words like anxious, depressed, angry, and guilty. Usually the patient can do this but sometimes they will come back with a word that is a bit vague like 'upset', and they have to be helped to a more specific emotion word. On other occasions they will reply with a thought, and one can then ask whether their reply is a thought or an emotion.) The clinician would then say, 'We have a situation, an emotion, and we now come to the very important part, and that's for you to consider the question "What would be going through the person's mind that led him to feel the emotion"' (emphasising the model). Hopefully the patient will say something like 'Right, the situation is that the person is being criticised by his boss and is feeling anxious, he'd probably be thinking "Oh God, I'm going to be sacked"'. (The thought 'I'll be sacked' would indeed be a good example of a negative automatic thought.)

The main issue in teaching patients this technique is to help them identify the 'key' or 'hot' thought. Sometimes asking the question about what the person is thinking about leads to an irrelevant thought, and it is important to help the patient 'inference chain' to the hot thought.

This could be done as follows, continuing with the example above:

Patient: 'He'd be anxious because he was criticised'
Clinician: 'What was he thinking about being criticised that makes him anxious?'
P: 'That he could lose his job?'
C: 'And if he did lose his job?'
P: 'He may become destitute?'

That last statement could well be the patient's hot thought, particularly if they experienced an unhealthy emotion when they thought it, or they thought it was their bottom line fear. It is quite important when doing the diary to try to get to the 'hot thought', though in practice it can be quite difficult to do.

One would then move on to the next section of the example that is being used, to explain the rationale for the diary:

Clinician: 'If the person who was criticised felt anxious, how would he respond in a behavioural way?' (Reinforcing the model.)
Patient: 'He might start avoiding work tasks, he may over-check his work, he might seek reassurance from his colleagues that he is doing the right thing'
C: 'That sounds right, and some of these behaviours may not be helpful'

Patients may not give such a 'textbook answer' and it may be necessary to discuss it further using Socratic dialogue to aid understanding. The clinician should then go on to seek the link between other emotions, thoughts and behaviours, linked in to the one triggering situation. She could ask 'What other emotion might a person feel when they were criticised by their manager?' In this situation the clinician would take the patient through the other emotions that they would be likely to feel, and draw from the patient what the likely thoughts and behaviours would be. The questions described above would be asked.

The clinician would then ask what the point of the example was. The patient would hopefully understand that it shows that you can react in different ways to the same situation. If the patient does not understand this, then the point would have to be discussed further to aid understanding. Examples other than being criticised could be used, and the practiced therapist would have a variety of examples to make this point. The patient would then be shown the diary that they would be asked to fill in. There are a variety of diaries in different books and one that can be photocopied is given in Appendix 5.1.

We would give a copy of this diary to the patient and allow them to briefly familiarise themselves with the layout. We would give advice on how to complete the diary, the main points being:

1   Noticing a change in emotions should be the trigger to fill the diary in. Patients should therefore go away from the session being much more alert to these changes. It may be helpful to discuss the first signs that they notice when their emotions change.
2   The diary should be completed at the time when there is an emotional disturbance and not later. If it is done later then the emotion has gone and there is little engagement with the experience. Obviously doing the diary at the time can be a bit impractical and we will discuss this later.
3   The diary should always be filled in and it is much less desirable for the patient just to do the exercise in their heads. There really seems to be something lost when it is not written down. It may be more permissible for the patient to not write it down when they have mastered the technique.

4   One must reassure the patient that it is not a test or exam, and that it may take some time to 'get the hang of it'.

One must address any reservations or concerns that the patient has about doing the technique. The typical anxious thoughts that the patient may have about doing the diary are as follows:

- *'It's a bit like homework from school'.* It would be said that the most important changes are going to be made in the patient's own environment, so it is most important that these between session tasks are completed. It is important to ensure that the process is very collaborative, as that comment would imply that the task is being imposed in a patronising manner. The term homework would be abandoned and a phrase (which may be preferable) like 'inter-session task' or a phrase of the patient's choosing would be used.
- *'I'll get it wrong/make spelling/grammar mistakes'.* It would be stated that the grammar or spelling is not important and will not be criticised. Likewise, there is not an absolutely right way of doing it; it is a tool to help the patient. It would be explained that most people take some time to get skilled at the procedure, but generally do find it very helpful.
- *'If people see me filling it in they'll realise I've got a problem'.* This could indeed be a real issue, and it would be suggested that the patient transfer the format of the diary to a more inconspicuous format like a personal organiser or an A4 notepad. If this were not practical then it would be suggested that they take themselves out of the situation for a short time (to another more private room).
- *'I can't see the point of doing it'.* The rationale of doing the exercise would be explained again and their concerns would be dealt with. The patient would be asked to set it up as a behavioural experiment to test out her reservations about the diary. However a comment like this may suggest a significant anxiety about the strong emotion that they may have to face, or a lack of engagement with the CBT process.
- *'I'm not sure that I've got time to do it'.* There may be some truth in this or it may mask underlying concerns that need to be explored. It would be enquired how much impact the problem was having in their life. It may be that the work required is too much to overcome a problem with only a small impact.
- *'How many negative thoughts do you want me to write?'* The answer to this is, strictly speaking, the amount the patient actually has. Obviously if the patient is very distressed it may be excessively onerous to ask them to be filling in diaries all day. It may therefore be reasonable to set a limit of say three or four entries a day. On average people bring back 1–3 entries from most days and this is reasonable.

The question arises whether one should, after explaining the first part of the diary linking situations, emotions and negative thoughts, go straight on to explain the second page of the diary, which is concerned with challenging the thoughts. Obviously this explanation either needs to be done at that time or it could be explained later when the person has completed examples of the first page. The normal procedure would be that one would first review the patient's diaries from the first exercise. We would try to help them improve their use of the diary: there is not usually a problem with filling in the first column. Regarding the second column about emotion, patients usually can identify the appropriate emotion in that situation. Sometimes they (as we described in the example above) have several emotional responses to the one situation and of course this is quite acceptable in terms of the diary format. The important thing is to help them appreciate that the negative thoughts that lead to one emotion will be different to those that lead to the other emotion (e.g. 'I'll lose my job and be destitute' leading to anxiety, and 'I'm a failure' leading to depression). In terms of the format it is important to separate the different thoughts leading to different emotions into different columns. There is often a lot of difficulty in deciding what the key/hot thought is, and indeed there may not be just one, there may be two thoughts of equal emotionality.

A lot of time would be taken explaining how to actually challenge the negative thoughts, which is the second page of the diary; the patient would be taken through this. The first column is 'Supporting the negative thought', and it would be explained that this is where evidence that supports the thought should be placed. The next and most important column is 'Challenging the negative thought'. It would be suggested to the patient that there are five questions that are of particular importance, and they are:

1   *'What evidence does not support the hot thought?'* Here we are looking for any specific factual evidence that does not support the thought. Going back to the example above the person may write, 'I'm not likely to lose my job as all my appraisals up to now have been good'; 'It's not possible to be sacked on the basis of one small mistake'; 'If my boss wants to discipline me then there is a procedure to go through'; 'Other people have made this mistake and nothing much has happened to them'; 'Even if I lost my job I would not become destitute as I have some savings'.

2   *'Is there another way of thinking about the situation?'* The patient should try to look at the situation from another angle. 'Maybe the boss is having a bad day'; 'That criticism isn't fully justified'; 'He's under pressure from his own boss and is letting off steam'.

3   *'Why is it not helpful to think like this?'* Here we are looking at the effect negative thinking can have on the patient's emotions, behaviour, physical state, interpersonal functioning, and so on. 'It's not helping me because I'm feeling anxious, which is leading me to feel dizzy and tired, and this is stopping me completing my work schedules'. 'It also makes me over check my work to ensure I've not made a mistake, which is also slowing me down'. 'It's making me stop talking to my boss and that isn't helping our relationship'.

4   *'What would I say to my best friend who was thinking like this?'* Again this
is to help the patient become detached from his emotional involvement, and
look at things objectively. 'I'll tell my friend that: getting criticised isn't the
end of the world, and we all make mistakes; if he had made a genuine mistake he should try to learn from the experience; if he feels that the criticism
is not justified he should discuss his concerns with his boss'.

5   *'Am I making a "thinking error"? Which one?'* Get the patient to review the
list of thinking errors and decide whether this has occurred. This is a slightly
different challenge than the others in that it is directed to the person's thinking style, rather than content of their thoughts. Therapists and patients vary
in how helpful they find this tactic of being aware of thinking style, but it is
certainly worth trying. 'I'm catastrophising – I'm looking for the worst possible outcome, which is unlikely to happen' could be a useful response here.

The next thing to do is to arrive at a 'balanced thought'. This is a thought that
is an alternative to the original 'hot thought' that is more realistic and helpful
(though occasionally realism may conflict with helpfulness). The patient should
write out the thought in a relatively short sentence. Most patients will understand
this concept fairly quickly and provide good examples. However you may need to
help them by asking 'Could you say, in a sentence, what would be a better thought
than the original hot thought?' The patient should then re-rate their strength of
belief as a percentage score. If they score poorly (perhaps below 50 per cent), then
they may need to be asked why they are not more convinced of it, as one would
expect of them having done the exercise. We would then ask them to re-rate the
emotional response as a percentage.

When the patient has arrived at the balanced thought then there is an issue
about what to do with that thought. It is not likely to be helpful to work with
all of the negative thoughts, particularly as there may be quite a few. We would
suggest that focus is directed to those thoughts that have an emotional meaning
for the patient, or that have a link to the formulation, or where the patient is very
obviously engaged with the process of working with the thought. If the patient
expresses little emotion, if the therapist can see little link with the formulation,
or if the patient seems distracted or 'going through the motions' then it is unhelpful to do any further work with the thought. By 'further work' we mean helping
someone discover whether the balanced thought is true; this would likely to be
by conducting a behavioural experiment or a survey to elicit this information.
This process will now be described below. If the person does accept, then or
later, that the balanced thoughts are true then it is important that the person is
able to think this in any future stressful situation. This is done partly by writing
the statement on 'flashcards', which are cards with the balanced thought written
on them.

The use of negative thought diaries with CFS patients

Examples of negative thoughts that CFS patients have are:

* 'I'll not be able to cope/I can't cope'
* 'I'll never get better'
* 'I'm useless'
* 'I'm a failure'
* 'No one understands me'
* 'These symptoms will get worse and worse'
* 'If I exercise I'll be crippled'

Rules and beliefs

As described in Chapter 2, there are three levels of thinking, namely thoughts, rules, and beliefs: rules and beliefs will be dealt with in this section. By beliefs we mean attitudes that are ingrained, absolute and very strongly held. They are not at all easy to change. They can be beliefs about oneself, usually of a self-depreciatory nature, beliefs about other people, and beliefs about the future. Examples would be 'I'm weak', 'Other people will take advantage of me', and 'I will always be exploited'.

Different CBT theorists define 'belief' in different ways; Beck (1976) emphasises the idea of 'schema' as cognitive structures that organise and give meaning to experiences that occur. He would therefore advocate the idea of, for example, an 'unworthiness schema' that may contain beliefs, emotions, bodily sensations and motivational factors. A part of that schema would be the core belief 'I'm no good'. Similarly Young (1994) uses the idea of early maladaptive schemas for his 'schema focused' work with personality disorder. He would see schemas as unconditional, not immediately available to consciousness, latent, functional or dysfunctional, compelling to various degrees, and pervasive or narrow depending on to what extent they influence the person's life (Wills and Sanders 1997).

Young, Klosko and Weishaar (2003) identify particular schemas that are similar to those often seen in CFS. They have a schema domain of 'other directedness' in which they identify a 'subjugation' schema and a 'self-sacrifice' schema. A 'subjugation schema' describes surrendering control to others because one feels coerced, and one is trying to avoid anger, retaliation and abandonment; needs and emotions can both be suppressed. They describe an association with psychosomatic disorder. A 'self-sacrifice schema' describes voluntarily meeting the needs of others at the expense of oneself, to avoid feeling selfish or causing pain, and to connect to needy others. In the schema domain of 'over-vigilance and inhibition' they identify 'unrelenting standards/hyper-criticalness', the belief that it is necessary to meet extremely high standards of behaviour and performance usually to avoid criticism. This leads to a sense of pressure and difficulty in slowing down. They also describe 'emotional inhibition' of spontaneity, to avoid disapproval, shame and a sense of losing control. In the schema domain of 'impaired autonomy and performance' they describe 'failure' as a belief that this is what you are in relation to your peers (Young et al 2003). They postulate that you are likely to respond to the schema by surrendering to it, by avoiding it, or by overcompensation in response to it.

So it is important to remember that there is little research on whether patients have these beliefs/schemas. However, as we have seen there is some mixed evidence that CFS patients have perfectionistic traits. Anthony and Swinson (1998) describe characteristic beliefs and behaviour in perfectionism in their excellent self-help book. The behaviours they identify are: overcompensation, going too far to get it right; excessive checking and reassurance seeking; repeating and correcting; excessive organising and list making; procrastinating, and having difficulty making decisions; not knowing when to quit or giving up too soon; being too slow; failing to delegate; hoarding; avoidance; excessively trying to change others. These behaviours would be divided into those that help the person try to meet their perfectionistic standards, and those that help the person avoid having to live up to those standards. These behaviours can maintain beliefs because they are stopping the person learning that they do not have to be so perfectionistic.

Rules and assumptions are at an equivalent level in terms of thinking. Rules, sometimes called imperatives or 'shoulds', are not usually at the forefront of awareness but can easily be brought there. They are rules about how the individual will act, often across a variety of domains. Examples are 'I should always... avoid risks... put other people first... praise myself... do things perfectly'. The list would be long. These rules are addressed in therapy because they are not necessarily 'wrong', but they are held and applied in a way that is too inflexible and is overall unhelpful to the person.

Assumptions are 'if... then' statements. For example: 'If a girl looks at me closely, then she'll see I'm ugly', 'If someone gives me a compliment then they are being kind and don't really mean it', 'If my partner even glances at another woman, then it means he must fancy her'. They are therefore statements often about specific events, which indicate the consequences of those events. They often lead on to rule statements. For example with the statement 'If a girl looks at me closely she'll see I'm ugly' it would follow '...so I *should never* get close to a girl'. All of these assumptions and rules will lead to patterns of behaviour. For example the rule 'I should always put other people first' may lead to behaviours such as always agreeing to demands, failing to be assertive, helping others to an exhausting degree, and so on.

A key issue is the relationship between beliefs, rules and negative thoughts. It is generally accepted that beliefs and rules are fundamental and that negative thoughts arise from them, but the negative thoughts also have a role in reinforcing and maintaining them, as of course do the associated behaviours. Similarly the rules may, in a sense, 'stand alone' without there being a clear dysfunctional belief; a person may just believe that they should do things perfectly as this was strongly emphasised to them as a child, and they do not believe it has major consequences for them or says anything about them as a person if they do not do things perfectly. Usually, however, the rule has a clear relationship with a belief, often a defensive relationship, in that whilst the rule is being followed then the core belief with its associated emotion is not in the person's immediate awareness. One needs therefore to tread warily when working with rules.

If a person has the core belief 'Deep down, I'm weird and horrible', they then may develop the assumption 'If people get to know me well they'll realise this, therefore I *should* avoid all intimacy'. The behavioural pattern is to avoid getting close to people, which reduces their skills at social interaction, and reduces their ability to make friends; they have frequent negative thoughts ('No one likes me', 'I can't talk to people', 'I'm an outsider') and these thoughts lead to a reinforcement of their belief, depression and further behavioural disturbances.

It is clear that dysfunctional schemas and rules will be present in people with personality disorders but may also be present in people with what the 'Diagnostic and Statistical Manual' would call Axis I Disorders (American Psychiatric Association 1995). These are theoretically complex areas and beyond the scope of this text; see Wills and Sanders (1997) for a fuller discussion.

When to work with rules and beliefs

The conventional wisdom when treating straightforward disorders is to work initially with thoughts, and then to spend some sessions, if necessary, working with rules and beliefs with a relapse prevention rationale. There is a certain lack of sense here, because if these deeper cognitive processes need more sessions the work should not be allocated just a few sessions at the end of therapy. In terms of evidence based practice the research is inconclusive (Jacobson, Dobson, Truax et al 1996). In actual clinical situations with CFS patients it is the author's experience that it is useful to work at this level quite early. There may be a case for working at this level and bypassing the negative thought level; this needs to be judged on an individual basis. (The evidence base, however, does not provide much evidence as to whether it is helpful to work with rules/beliefs in CFS.)

Working with rules and beliefs

In Chapter 3 on assessment an explanation was given as to how to discover a patient's rules and beliefs. In terms of beliefs the method was: to 'inference chain' from negative thoughts; to ask specific questions about how the person sees himself, the world or other people, and the future; to pay close attention to the person's strong emotional experiences; and to do questionnaires like the Young Schema Questionnaire (Young and Brown 2001). In terms of rules the method was: to look for particular behavioural patterns and enquire about rules that may drive these; and to listen out for rule statements such as 'I must...' and 'If that happened then...'.

Challenging rules

The first stage is to get the wording right, to ensure that the rule that you have agreed upon and written down is one that 'rings true' to the patient. A photocopyable workbook is provided in Appendix 5.2 to help the clinician work with rules and beliefs. (It is based on Greenberger and Padesky 1995 and Fennell 1999.) Some clinicians use different forms for rules and for beliefs, but one type of form can cover both. (This form is the equivalent of the negative thought diary described earlier in the chapter.)

Procedure and clinical example

Write the rule at the top of the sheet. Check with the person that they agree that the rule is to some degree unhelpful or unreasonable. If the person does not agree with this then discuss their strong allegiance to the rule, suggesting ways in which it does not always serve them. The majority of patients will go along with this approach. Explain the rationale for doing this work, by saying, for example: 'Thinking back to the formulation that we did, you'll remember that we identified rules that were contributing to the problem. What I'd like to do now is to do some work on these, trying to make them more flexible and helpful to you. It is important to say that we are not attacking your personality. We all have rules, most of which are helpful; it is important however to recognise how certain unhelpful rules contribute to the problems that you are having. It may be that the rules developed when you were younger to help you deal with a situation but they are less relevant now. What do you think of doing this?'

Start working through the questions on the form, asking the patient to read and respond to the questions. This has to be a slow and sensitive process, remembering that patients have adhered to these rules for a long time.

WHAT IS THE OLD RULE OR BELIEF?

Patient: 'I must always do things perfectly'.

WHERE DID THE RULE OR BELIEF COME FROM AND HOW HAS IT BEEN REINFORCED OVER THE YEARS?

Patient: 'My dad was a very successful businessman and had very high expectations of us, in all areas of our life. He was also quite critical, particularly of me, in comparison to my sisters who seemed to be prettier and cleverer. I took his criticisms to heart and it knocked my self-esteem. I felt the only way to get more love and praise from my dad was to be the best in absolutely everything and I guess I'm still like that.'

It can be quite difficult and emotional for the patient to explore the basis of their assumption. However it is important to have a full discussion of key factors. These may be parental attitudes, cultural and religious values, school experiences or relationships: sometimes the patient needs some encouragement in talking about these things. It can also help to explore the way that the rules have been reinforced, which can be a subtler issue: for example the way that the successful implementation of the rule leads to a reward, or the way that the rule stops the person acting in another way that stops them learning that the other way may be better.

WHAT EFFECT HAS THE RULE OR BELIEF HAD ON YOUR LIFE?

Patient: 'I think when I was younger I used to work very hard at school. It probably helped me get good A levels. When I got a job it led me to always want to be the best, to get promotion, and so on. More negatively it makes me set fantastic, unrealistic standards for myself. Having to be top saleswoman, never making mistakes… it's very tiring. Even if I achieve these things I'm not happy. The main advantage is that in some ways it helps me be successful at work; I've reached quite a senior position that gives me a good income.'

The therapist should acknowledge the benefits of the rule but, if appropriate, ask if they are genuine benefits. Otherwise questions should be asked about the historic and current disadvantages of thinking like this. The clinician should acknowledge that the rule may have advantages, but should ask whether the advantages would occur if the person believed a modified version of the rule: for example, instead of believing that she must always do things perfectly, to have believed that she should aim to do her best but accept that sometimes it will be impossible to achieve. The clinician should always ask what the patient's concerns are about giving up the rule.

HOW DO I KNOW THE RULE OR BELIEF IS ACTIVE?

Patient: 'I feel particularly tired. I also feel stressed if I'm aiming for something like a sales target and possibly not reaching it. I can get a bit irritable with my boyfriend if he's getting in the way of what I want to do.'

It is important to draw out as many factors as possible and relate them specifically to the rule.

WHAT IS THE EVIDENCE THAT THE RULE OR BELIEF IS NOT COMPLETELY TRUE?

Patient: 'I'm not sure, possibly because it's impossible to do things perfectly. Or there's no such thing as perfection. In real life you've got to prioritise things.'

Here it is important to get as many arguments as possible that show that the rule is unrealistic. Typical questions would be:

• In what way is this rule unrealistic?

- Is there a law that says you have to accept this?
- What would the world be like if everyone thought like this?

WHY IS THIS RULE OR BELIEF UNHELPFUL TO ME?

Patient: 'I feel very stressed, anxious. I don't take enough time to rest. Possibly family life suffers a bit because I'm always late at work.'

Again the therapist can ask a range of questions to elicit unhelpful side effects. For example:

- 'What adverse effect does the rule have on your mood, your thinking, your behaviour, your relationships, your work, etc. (at the moment and in the past)?'
- 'How would you advise your best friend if they always followed this rule?'

The patient should be given a homework task of collecting evidence on a daily basis that runs contrary to the old belief or rule.

WHAT IS THE NEW RULE OR BELIEF?

Patient: 'I'll aim to do my best if it is an important issue. I will have to prioritise issues and may not be able to give 100 per cent effort.'

At this stage it is important to discuss with the patient what the new rule should be. It should reflect flexibility, therefore should express a 'preference' rather than a 'must'; it should lead to outcomes that are beneficial to the patient; it should be a statement that the person is happy to try to work on accepting; it should not be a statement that is too long and convoluted; it should reflect that following the rule is not likely to lead to disastrous outcomes.

PROVIDE FURTHER EVIDENCE THAT THE NEW RULE OR BELIEF IS MORE REALISTIC AND HELPFUL

Patient: 'Since I've been trying to follow it I haven't being staying so late. I've been getting slightly behind with my work but it's manageable. I was spending a lot of time before checking that I've not made mistakes, and it hasn't led to more mistakes.'

DEVISE BEHAVIOURAL CHANGES THAT TEST OR SUPPORT THE NEW RULE OR BELIEF

This is fundamentally important and is a process of moving the patient from a lightly held 'intellectual' acceptance of the rule, to a firmly held 'emotional' acceptance of the rule.

The key factor here will be devising behavioural changes or experiments in which the person acts in accordance with the new rule. For example:

1   I will finish work at 6pm on at least four days out of five.
2   When I am doing a final draft of my essay I will take no longer than three hours.
3   When I am studying my university course I will not procrastinate. I will start working within five minutes of sitting at the desk.
4   Next month I will aim to be the second top salesperson and not the first as I usually do.

The helpfulness and acceptability of the behaviours and the effect on the new rule would be reviewed every session.

Core beliefs

As the definition suggests, these are beliefs that the patient holds that are 'core' to their sense of self. These are beliefs about themselves, other people (or how the world works), and the future. The most important beliefs are likely to be the ones the patient has about themselves, and these may include 'I'm lazy', 'I'm stupid', 'I'm a failure', 'I'm bad', 'I'm evil'. Core beliefs are likely to have developed in childhood or adolescence, particularly in response to abusive situations. They may develop because the child finds it easier to blame herself than consider the alternative view that her parents are untrustworthy. As the child gets older they may or may not be re-evaluated and modified (Greenberger and Padesky 1995). One may therefore encounter an adult who accepts extremely self-critical beliefs in an unconditional way.

When to work with core beliefs

If it was clear from one's formulation that the patient's core beliefs were contributing, by whatever mechanism, to their symptoms, then working at this level would be indicated. This would be likely to happen in a minority of cases, whereas working with rules and assumptions is more common.

Eliciting core beliefs

This subject was covered in detail in Chapter 3 on assessment. To briefly re-iterate, the methods would be to inference chain from negative thoughts, to ask specific questions about the patient's view of themselves, the world and the future, to explore areas of strong emotion, and to use questionnaires.

Testing core beliefs

This needs to be done sensitively as we are asking the patient to face up to a view of themselves that they would normally avoid or find distressing. The main approaches to testing core beliefs are by recording experiences that are inconsistent with the old core belief and consistent with a new core belief, rating confidence in the new belief, conducting behavioural experiments to test the new beliefs, and doing a historical test of the new belief (see Greenberger and Padesky 1995 for a full description). It may also be the case that work has to be done with imagery, in session relationship work, and even limited re-parenting in complex cases and personality disorders (Young et al 2003). It will take much longer to weaken core beliefs than it will negative thoughts, so the therapist must help the patient do the exercises slowly but consistently over perhaps a year.

A fundamental difference between working with negative thoughts and beliefs however is the considerable amount of repetition that is required to shift some of these ingrained ideas, and the ingenuity and persistence that the patient and therapist have to display on using behavioural, emotional and cognitive approaches in weakening these beliefs. Appropriate strategies would be:

- Acting in accordance with the new belief for at least a year to see some movement
- Repeated and forceful verbal support of the new belief
- Repeated surveys to gain support for the new beliefs (Young, Klosko and Weishaar 2003)
- Empty chair and role-play approaches particularly looking at formative experiences
- Historical log supporting new belief

The procedure for conducting behavioural experiments around beliefs and rules is the same as that described previously. As stated earlier, experiments may need to be conducted many times to shift very ingrained attitudes.

Apart from working with unhelpful thoughts and beliefs, other strategies for dealing with stressful life events are:

1   Using a problem solving approach as described in Chapter 7. This is a particularly good approach if the person is dealing with crises or dilemmas.
2   Trying to address factors that research demonstrates contributes to stress: help the patient to reduce being overloaded and overburdened; help them reduce the sense of being out of control; help them ensure that they have the appropriate support of others (Ogden 2004).
3   Using meditation as described in Chapter 7.
4   Removing oneself from the stress for a temporary or permanent period. If on the basis of the assessment it is obvious that a particular factor is tremendously stressful and clearly contributing to the symptoms then it may be

reasonable to discuss getting away from it if it is impossible to address it by other means. The most obvious thing here is the work situation.

Psychiatric disorder

If a person has an actual psychiatric disorder then it is possible to use medication, CBT and other approaches to help this. As stated in Chapter 1 it is known that CFS patients have a current (25 per cent) and lifetime (50–75 per cent) prevalence of depression. Generalised anxiety disorder and somatisation disorders occur more frequently in CFS patients than in the general population, usually preceding CFS symptoms. There are CBT protocols in other books that describe a treatment approach, for example Leahy and Holland's 'Treatment Plans and Interventions for Depression and Anxiety Disorders' (2000). The clinician working with the CFS patients may either be able to treat the person themselves using the CBT approach or refer the person on to an appropriate practitioner. How the treatment of the psychiatric disorder and the CFS interact with one another must depend on the information that is obtained from the assessment and formulation.

Chapter summary

Difficult life events can occur, and these can cause emotional problems and stress. It may be that the person is overloaded with repeated events but it is also important to think about how the person thinks, feels and behaves in response to them. The person with CFS may also suffer from depression, anxiety or another psychiatric disorder. Emotional problems and psychiatric disorders could be precipitating and maintenance factors for the CFS symptoms, so attempts should be made to help with these problems. Approaches used may be medication, psychiatric care, CBT, or ensuring the patient has a sense of control and adequate social support, and ensuring they are not overburdened.

Chapter 6

Helping patients with other factors that may maintain the symptoms

This chapter contains:

*   Helping patients work with other potential maintenance factors such as sleep problems, physical illness and viruses, iatrogenic factors, and disadvantages of recovering
*   Helping patients consider predisposing and precipitating factors

Sleep problems

It is common in patients who have CFS to describe sleep problems. Usually they describe not having adequate hours of sleep, or having adequate hours of sleep but feeling 'unrefreshed', or occasionally having excessive sleep. One large study (Unger, Nisenbaum, Moldofsky, Cesta, Sammut, Reyes and Reeve 2004) found that 81.4 per cent of CFS subjects had an abnormal sleep factor as measured by questionnaire. Other studies found that unrefresing sleep is the most common sleep abnormality, with 88–95 per cent in community studies (Jason, Richman, Rademaker, Jordan, Plioplys, Taylor, McCready, Huang and Plioplys 1999) and 70–80 per cent in clinic studies (Morriss, Sharpe, Sharpley, Cowen, Hawton and Morris 1993; Buchwald, Pascualy, Bombardier and Kith 1994). If one is not sleeping well then this will increase fatigue, cognitive problems and even joint pain and fitness (Unger et al 2004). The patients' subjective reports of sleep disturbance are not entirely supported by objective testing (see Chapter 1). It would seem reasonable that assessment of sleep using a standard diary should be completed on all patients who describe this problem (see Chapter 3).

Patients with depression as an additional problem will also commonly complain of insomnia, with difficulty falling asleep, frequent or prolonged waking through the night, and early morning wakening. Occasionally depressed people will complain of sleeping too much (Benca, Obermeyer, Shelton, Droster and Kalin 2000). Patients with anxiety disorders frequently have problems: sleep studies into various categories of anxiety disorder suggest sleep disruption, including difficulty getting to sleep, increased time awake, early morning wakening, decreased sleep efficiency and reduced total sleep (Benca et al 2000). As described in Chapter 1, CFS patients are more likely to be anxious and depressed.

Studies have not managed to clarify how much sleep, in general, people need: the average amount taken is eight hours and this reduces with age (Herbert 1997). Another important issue is that most psychoactive substances will affect sleep either because of the direct effect of the drug or because of withdrawal effects (Benca et al 2000). Also poor sleep hygiene can be the cause of sleep problems, and this would include daytime napping, coffee and alcohol before bedtime, excessive noise, light, distractions, and so on.

How can inadequate sleep problems be helped? Hypnotic drugs are frequently used but longer acting ones can cause morning lethargy and sleepiness, and shorter acting ones can cause rebound insomnia and daytime anxiety as part of a withdrawal syndrome. Clearly caution would have to be used here with CFS patients. Psychological therapy is effective, however, and a recent review indicated that 70–80 per cent of patients benefited (Espie 2002).

Cognitive behavioural therapy for sleep problems consists of some of the following elements:

- *Sleep education and hygiene.* Information about normal sleep is given, and the removal of bad sleep hygiene practices is planned out with the individual.
- *Stimulus control.* This idea is based on classical conditioning (association). It aims to ensure that the bed is purely associated with sleep, and that other domestic areas are not associated with sleep. It is suggested that patients should get up if they wake up and are in bed awake for more than 20 minutes; it is suggested that they should not do things like watch TV in bed, should not nap in the chair, and so on.
- *Cognitive control.* The person is asked to set aside 15 minutes at the end of the day to think through any unfinished business, and plan for tomorrow. It is aimed at reducing worrying.
- *Thought suppression.* The person is urged to sub-vocally articulate the word 'the' every three seconds. This is an attempt to block anxious thoughts.
- *Imagery and relaxation.*
- *Challenging negative thoughts*, as described in Chapter 5, but focussed on negative thoughts about sleep such as 'If I lose sleep I'll be completely unable to function'.

It has not been established which of these techniques has the most potency. A typical brief programme will be described here that may help the person with sleep problems:

1   Assess the duration and quality of sleep by means of a diary (see Chapter 3). Evaluate any interference with sleep arising from medication and substances such as alcohol, caffeine, benzodiazepines and SSRI anti-depressants. Assess poor sleep 'hygiene'. Evaluate unhelpful beliefs about sleep. Assess pain and emotional states that may interfere with sleep. Assess whether pain is keeping the person awake and/or waking them up. If this is the case the person

may benefit from analgesics, and the time, dose, and duration of effect should be discussed with the prescriber. (They may also benefit from the pain management techniques described in Chapter 7.)

2   Address poor sleep 'hygiene': is the patient's bedroom warm, comfortable, quiet and sleep friendly? Does the person they sleep with interfere with their own sleep (different bedtimes, snoring)? Does the issue of sex help or hinder their sleep? They may need advice that they should wind down for sleep and that heavy meals, vigorous exercise, and stimulating mental activity should be avoided.

3   Advise the patient that caffeine will keep them awake, alcohol will be likely to get them asleep but may lead to waking in the middle of the night, and that benzodiazepines may cause a 'rebound' effect. Help them think about altering the timing of these substances, stopping them or changing them. This may need to be discussed with their GP.

4   Frequently anxiety (often in the form of worry) and other emotions can interfere with sleep. Hopefully anxiety will be reduced if the person is correctly using the negative thought diary, or successfully addressing anxiety in another way. However, some people may have some significant problems and dilemmas that are difficult to switch off from. Sometimes the best that can be done is to ask the individuals to give themselves a 15-minute worry period and then to switch off from their worries at other times, possibly by using the sub-vocalising technique described above. In conjunction with this the patients could teach themselves a meditation or relaxation technique, and there are many available. Alternatively, the person could be asked to do an activity that they would normally find relaxing and absorbing (the absorbing factor may be important to reduce cognitive 'noise').

5   If the person has unhelpful thoughts and beliefs about sleep then they should be encouraged to challenge them. These may include: 'If I don't get x hours of sleep I'll not be able to function' and 'I'm sleeping very badly' (when the evidence contradicts this). The negative thought diary can be used here. Excessive attempts to force themselves to get to sleep should be challenged in the paradoxical way described above.

6   If none of this works then a stricter behavioural programme can be tried, as follows:

a   the rationale for the programme is explained in terms of creating an association between bed and being asleep and vice versa;

b   the patient is asked to go to bed and get up at the same time each evening to create an association with a particular bedtime;

c   if the person wakes through the night and they cannot get to sleep again within 20 minutes (the time is negotiable), then they should get up and not return to bed again until they are sleepy. This should be repeated every time they are awake for 20 minutes. An upper limit of trials of this strategy may be agreed;

d   the effects should be evaluated through diary keeping.

It is difficult to think of a specific intervention for those patients who sleep adequate hours but describe themselves as completely unrefreshed. In the related condition of fibromyalgia, 60–90 per cent of patients described non-restorative sleep: it was considered that this type of sleep was caused by a lack of deep sleep, and tricyclic anti-depressants were used with some beneficial effect (Reiffenberger and Amundson 1996). This may be something to consider for the CFS group who complain of being unrefreshed, as the same phenomenon may be occurring.

Oversleeping

For the patient who sleeps too much, again it is important to assess why this is occurring. Is the patient trying to escape something? Is the excessive sleep (over the standard eight hours) causing problems? Even if the patient is saying that it is not causing problems, it is normally considered a possible problem because excessive time in bed could breed further inactivity and may contribute to deconditioning: it may also affect the person's ability to sleep at night. It is a matter of judgement as to whether one should attempt to reduce this because the person may be catching up after a period of significant exhaustion. There may be an important difference between the person who for a few weeks is taking nine to ten hours to catch up, and the person who for months has been sleeping very excessively, the latter being problematic. If one is going to help the person reduce to, say, eight hours, then the most important thing is to do it gradually. For example the person could reduce by 15 minutes each week. Clinical experience would suggest that most patients could successfully do this.

Experience would suggest that if sleep can be improved then this can have an impact on symptoms, particularly fatigue symptoms.

Physical illness

As described in Chapter 2, there are a variety of physical problems that will have fatigue and pain as symptoms, including rheumatoid arthritis, lupus, cancer and other conditions. A complexity can arise if the patient is sent with a diagnosis of both a physical condition and CFS, though if the physical illness accounts for the fatigue then they should not be given the CFS diagnosis (see Chapter 1). It is possible to try to differentiate the physical symptoms of the medical condition from those of CFS and this can be aided by advice from the GP or physician: one would then try to treat those using the CBT approach. An alternative approach would be just to consider that some of the interventions that are used to help symptoms such as stress, sleep and deconditioning may have some beneficial effect on the medical condition if those symptoms are worsening the person's ability to cope with the medical condition. Cognitive behavioural therapy has been used for patients who have medical problems such as diabetes, cardiac disease, cancer and skin conditions (White 2001).

If CFS patients are obese, this may be a contributory factor towards their symptoms, through the possible mechanisms of poor nutrition or having to carry about extra weight. This can be addressed in terms of helping the patient lose weight. The author is not aware of research on obesity in CFS, but clinically has observed that in a few patients being overweight was likely to be contributing to their symptoms.

It is important with CFS patients in general to be alert for any particular patient who develops unusual or new symptoms, or ones that are hard to make sense of, or are not typical of CFS. If this happens the patient should be asked to return to their GP or physician to be checked over. An example of this would be a patient who started bleeding, was passing out or having fevers. With some of these symptoms it would be clear that further investigations were necessary, but with others it is more a matter of judgement. However it is possible that the patient could develop another physical illness whilst having CBT and obviously this should not be missed. Similarly if a patient is sent with 'probable CFS, awaiting investigations to rule out X', then it is probably wise not to see the patient until all other physical illnesses are excluded. Also if a referral is made for a patient who has a diagnosis of CFS, but on assessment the therapist cannot make any sense of the symptoms in terms of the predisposing/precipitating/maintenance model, then it is wise to send the patient back, indicating uncertainty about the diagnosis and possibly suggesting that the physician reconsiders the diagnosis. All these issues come up quite frequently, and there is further guidance from NICE (NICE 2006).

Frequent viruses

One of the many unpleasant experiences that CFS patients have to suffer is that of frequent viruses. This is a common complaint, and patients will usually say that it takes much longer to 'shake off' a virus once it has been caught. This is problematic, in one way just because of the unpleasantness of repeated colds/coughs/flu. More importantly these viruses significantly worsen fatigue, as they would for anyone, but the CFS sufferers are often very profoundly fatigued by viruses, more so than non-sufferers. It thus becomes a maintenance factor, possibly through mechanisms of the virus itself being fatiguing, and the impact of it leading to demoralisation and deconditioning. Patients describe the immune system being weakened, leading to frequent viruses, leading to a worsening of fatigue and other symptoms, leading to further viruses.

Can anything be done? One can advise patients to avoid people and situations where they are likely to pick up viruses – this could be people who are ill with viruses, hospitals, crowded places – and this advice may be more pertinent in winter, and the start of the school year. One can advise that they consider immunisation if this is possible. One could ask them to attend their GP in the early stages to see if anything can be done, though of course with most viruses symptom control rather than treatment is the goal. It is clear that it is impossible to completely stop people getting viruses, but for some badly affected people it is wise to see it as a maintenance factor and try to address it.

Iatrogenic factors

It is possible that iatrogenic factors (i.e. problems caused by medicine) may be significant as maintenance factors. Because the condition is complex and treatment protocols are unclear, then clinicians may give advice that is not always in the patient's best interest, or the patient may misunderstand the advice they are given. This situation is probably improving as the condition is more recognised. Examples that this author has encountered are:

- A GP telling a patient to rest in bed and, because he did not specify how long, the patient was still in bed two years later. The patient had significant problems with inactivity and deconditioning. This situation was not entirely the GP's fault.
- A very over-active patient with numerous demands on them, who was told by a clinician that activity was good for them. The patient took this to heart and started further activities and vigorous exercise that led to a complete collapse.
- A clinician misdiagnosed a patient with depression instead of CFS and prescribed a strong dose of anti-depressant that led to over-sedation in a patient who was already very drowsy and fatigued.
- An alternative medication practitioner who persuaded a patient to have all his fillings replaced at the cost of several thousand pounds, the only effect being financial stress.

The important thing here, to try to reduce iatrogenic effects, is to ensure that:

1 The maintenance factors are clearly assessed.
2 The patient is given specific and clear guidance as to what they should do.
3 Progress is monitored using objective measures, and treatment adjusted.
4 Evidence based practice is followed.

There is a need for guidelines and self-help materials to be used in treatment settings.

Disadvantages of recovering

It is important to say again that patients with CFS have to endure a large degree of suffering and that the vast majority are entirely focussed on getting better. However some patients' symptoms may be partly maintained by the disadvantages of recovering. It may even be that some patients fit better into the idea of somatisation. Somatisation is a psychiatric concept that describes the patient who has multiple physical symptoms without a clear cause, and the significance of the word is that emotional distress is turned ('somatised') into physical distress. It is argued that some of these patients may be searching for aid, seeking attention, seeking the sick role, trying to manipulate others or gaining something (Kellner 1991). It is possible that interest shown by family members and care systems can reinforce symptoms (Kellner 1991).

Are these factors relevant for CFS patients? In terms of insurance benefits it is only recently that CFS has been more recognised, and it is actually very hard for patients to meet criteria for significant benefit payment in the UK, such as Disability Living Allowance. Some patients are lucky enough to be in an insurance scheme that they can try to claim from.

Clinical experience suggests that occasionally patients' symptoms can be maintained partly because of these issues. Insurance and benefits can be a factor, and this is often associated with not going back to work; this usually occurs with a patient for whom work has been terribly demanding or stressful. Being in an insurance scheme allows them to safely opt out of this situation. This may be happening at or below the patients' level of awareness. In terms of receiving attention from health care systems, this is unlikely to be a factor, because it is very difficult for patients to get appropriate attention. In some cases there is a complicated effect on family systems. If a patient has some tendency to be anxious or dependent this may be reinforced by the attention they get by being sick. Often the dynamic is of a patient who has been extremely self-sacrificing, and for whom being in a legitimate physical illness role is the only way to be heard or get their needs met.

What is the best way to deal with these issues? Following the CBT model it is suggested that the clinician builds trust with the patient and if he thinks that these factors are significant he is direct with the patient about this. This will sometimes bring a response of angry denial, either because the person is aware and finds it painful to be honest about it, or he is unaware and becomes angered at the very suggestion. Other patients are able to be honest and will accept that they have got into a 'sick role', or are anxious about getting better. (This does not preclude them also suffering from the symptoms.)

Often the way forward is to explore these issues in depth, and often look at the pros and cons of their illness behaviour. Sometimes the patient's illness behaviour seems like a logical one in their circumstances, indeed almost the only thing they could do. For the patient to explore these issues with you they need to be confident that you will not communicate with the family/benefit/insurance scheme in a way that will disadvantage them.

Predisposing and precipitating factors

Predisposing and precipitating factors may or may not be able to be dealt with. Predisposing factors may be genetic, but may be personality structures in the form of beliefs to do with perfectionism/self-sacrifice, etc. This issue was addressed in Chapter 5.

Occasionally patients describe sexual and other abuse, of varying degrees of severity: a judgement must be made with the patient as to whether this should be worked with, and this could be through CBT or possibly other therapies. A complex issue here is whether the distress that this work could produce would have a detrimental effect on the symptoms, in the hope of gaining long term benefit. The author is not aware of any research in this subject.

Precipitating factors may be physical illnesses/stress/other demands, and sometimes these continue into being maintenance factors. Clinical experience suggests that sometimes traumatic events occur, before or after onset of CFS, and this can lead the person to develop post-traumatic stress disorder; if this has happened then there are ways to help the person through CBT or medication (Roth and Fonagy 1996). When doing the 'relapse prevention' element of the therapy (see Chapter 7) it is important to help the person understand precipitating factors in order that the patient can try to prevent relapse in the future.

Chapter summary

It is important to help patients with the other maintenance factors. Regarding sleep, most CFS patients describe problems with sleeping or the quality of their sleep, though sleep studies have not shown clear abnormalities. This problem should be assessed and if present treated by CBT, or possibly medication. Occasionally patients need to be helped with oversleeping. Looking at physical illness, it can complicate treatment if the patient has a co-existing physical disease. Therapists also need to be alert to the possibility that the CFS sufferer could develop a disease. Obesity can occasionally be a problem. Patients often complain of frequently picking up viruses that contribute to their fatigue. Occasionally patients are given poor health advice. Another less common maintenance factor is that there may be disadvantages in getting better.

Chapter 7

Managing pain and other problems arising from chronic fatigue syndrome

This chapter contains:

- Helping patients with other problems and symptoms including: pain, poor attention and memory, irritable bowel symptoms, CFS symptoms' impact on activities of daily living
- Maintaining progress
- Adjusting to the disorder

These problems are being discussed because they are reasonably common and because it may be possible to address them from a CBT perspective. Some symptoms that patients describe, such as 'heat and cold' sensitivity, are difficult to manage using the CBT model.

After the above problems have been considered the chapter will conclude with a discussion about when to end treatment, and how to ensure progress is maintained (sometimes called 'relapse prevention').

Pain

Pain is a common symptom described by CFS sufferers (Buchwald 1996; Buchwald and Garrity 1994). Patients often describe pain that is like an ache, but which can also be sharp. It often occurs in multiple sites in the body: for example in the back, radiating down to the legs, and in the wrists. Sometimes the pain disappears completely for periods, but for most sufferers it is always there, but can differ in intensity.

> *Patient example*: Alice's pain was fairly typical of CFS sufferers. 'It feels like a real ache, a bit like a toothache. I've got it in my legs worst of all but also in my back and neck. I would say it was always there but it definitely gets worse if I tire myself doing things like gardening or walking. If I walk more than a couple of hundred yards I will suffer. Stress can make it worse but that's not the main factor.'

It is useful to consider whether the pain comes on at the same times as the fatigue, as this would indicate it was being influenced by the same factors. Patients differ in terms of which symptom they find the most unpleasant but it is usually fatigue or pain.

The chronic pain literature is strongly influenced by behavioural theory, and also the theory of 'gate control'. Behavioural theory emphasises learning: an example of this would be operant learning, in which if the person engaged in activity that is punished (by significant pain) then it is likely to be stopped, but if the activity were rewarded in some way it is likely to be repeated. A patient could potentially be rewarded by being active, by the encouragement of his family, or from the care and attention he gets from his family whilst ill. This could lead to quite different patterns of behaviour.

The gate theory of pain (Melzack and Wall 1965, 1982) suggests that the pain 'gate' can be opened or closed depending on various factors, and that pain is a complex brain-determined event, rather than being a simple sensory phenomenon. When the gate is closed the patient experiences less pain, and there is more pain when it is opened. The gate can start to be shut by physical means, for example medication, but also by the way that pain is sensed and perceived, its implications judged, and how it is acted upon (Eimer and Freeman 1998). Often the goal is not so much to try to get the pain to go away completely, but to influence the factors described here, so that although the person still may have some pain, the 'suffering' element is reduced (Eimer and Freeman 1998). The strategies described here are similar to those described earlier: in the detailed assessment it is important to ensure that the pain element is fully understood, particularly the way the person reacts cognitively, behaviourally and emotionally to the pain. One can use specific questionnaires and diaries to tease out this symptom (see Eimer and Freeman 1998), or one can simply use a visual analogue scale of 0–8 for the patient to rate the severity and duration of his pain on a daily basis. Typical cognitive distortions that can occur in pain patients are:

- 'I am either in pain or not in pain'. This is a type of black or white thinking that disallows the patients from seeing progress
- 'There's no point in doing anything as I'll still be in pain'. This is a 'disqualifying the positive' type of thinking that can lead to low mood and lack of motivation, and avoidant behaviour.
- 'If I exercise or even move I could cripple myself'. This is a catastrophising type of thinking that can lead to anxiety, over-focus on pain, and avoidant and overcautious behaviours, with the potential for deconditioning. The pain literature would emphasise the importance of this issue.
- 'I can't bear this pain'. This is a type of thinking, often called 'low frustration tolerance' (Ellis 1962), in which the person tells himself that the pain is unbearable and intolerable when there is no objective evidence that this is the case.
- 'I'll always be in pain and nobody can help me'. This is over-generalisation

from one unpleasant instance to a global view as to how things will be. Plainly this can lead to depression and giving up.

The underlying assumptions and core beliefs related to perfectionism, people pleasing and self-criticism may also impact on pain. Usually this would be because the person ignores the pain too much in his attempts to push on and help others. It may also be stressful to follow these behavioural traits.

Not all CFS patients have these distortions and often their appraisal of their pain is realistic. It is possible that working with the maintenance factors described earlier may start to relieve all symptoms, but it may be necessary to address pain and other factors separately. It may be wise to assess the response to pain symptoms separately from the response to fatigue symptoms. It is possible that someone may push on in a perfectionistic way through fatigue symptoms but may become anxious and avoidant in the face of pain, and vice versa. The management of pain symptoms is similar to that of fatigue symptoms at a behavioural level with the use of pacing and graded activity (Eimer and Freeman 1998).

A particular issue that may need to be considered with pain is the use of pain-killing medication, and whether this is appropriate. Clinical experience is that CFS patients do not always find painkilling drugs very helpful, but they do not usually misuse them. Signs of a problem with drug use may include; chaotic drug use, opiate use or demands for this, or conversely strong aversion to taking analgesics when it is strongly indicated. The literature would suggest that these drugs should be taken on a regular rather than an *ad hoc* way, to ensure that the analgesic effect is fully experienced (Eimer and Freeman 1998).

The main additional strategy that is used when patients have pain is relaxation/ meditation/imagery/hypnosis. Clinical experience indicates that these are useful in some or most CFS patients.

Hypnosis has been used in chronic pain for some time, and has been described as 'a success story' (Heap and Aravind 2001). Hypnosis has two inter-related elements. The first one is that of suggestion, defined as: 'a communication, conveyed verbally by the hypnotist, that directs the subject's imagination in such a way as to elicit intended alterations in sensations, perceptions, feelings, thoughts and behaviours' (Heap and Aravind 2001). The second element is that of being in a trance: a waking state where the person is absorbed by internal experiences, and away from their surroundings. Hypnosis involves an interaction between these two experiences. It is likely that the pain relief obtained from hypnosis is gained from relaxation, distraction and de-catastrophising suggestions. In terms of the research that has been done with hypnosis, a meta-analysis suggested that hypnosis does have demonstrable efficacy in the treatment of pain (Hawkins 2001). Further details of how to integrate hypnosis with CBT can be found in Heap and Aravind (2001) and Eimer and Freeman (1998).

Imagery work is similar to hypnosis in the sense that the person enters an altered state of consciousness, though the suggestion element is absent. Again this work can be done to counter distressing physical pain. The person is asked whether there is an image that repeatedly occurs alongside of the pain; typical responses are 'burning', 'stinging' or 'toothache', and the patient can be asked to evoke an image of their pain. An alternative image is derived, for example cool wind, ice, soothing cream or being on a beach, and the person is asked to evoke this alternative image slowly using all five senses, until the old image is replaced and the pain reduces. This could take 15–20 minutes. The person is then asked to practise this once or twice a day, and when the pain breaks through. The mechanisms of this are likely to be reduction in muscle tension and increased distraction.

Distraction can be used as a treatment strategy in its own right, the rationale being that if one perceives and attends to pain it is likely to be worse (Eimer and Freeman 1998). An important point to make here is that with acute pain it is important to attend to it and decide how to manage it, but with chronic pain this attention to pain process is still very active but in a way in which nothing is gained (Eimer and Freeman 1998). A helpful strategy is to teach the patients to recognise the first signs of pain and then to quickly absorb themselves in another activity. It is important that the activity is significantly absorbing, and this could be an imagery or hypnosis exercise, or a general activity like a conversation, a computer game or cooking a meal. This strategy appeals to patients as it is intuitive, and something they probably have been trying themselves.

In recent years meditation has become important in CBT. There has been an important trial describing the effectiveness of mindfulness meditation in preventing relapse in depression (Teasdale, Segal, Williams, Ridgeway, Soulsby and Lau 2000). Also, Jon Kabatt-Zinn strongly advocates the use of mindfulness meditation to deal with stress and pain. He has run a course at the University of Massachusetts medical centre helping patients with pain and illness and has attempted to integrate that approach with modern medical and scientific knowledge. His approach is to help patients focus their attention on the breath, and away from bodily sensations. If the patient's attention comes off their breath (as observed in the nostrils, chest and belly), then they are instructed to bring their attention back to the breath. When any thought appears, it is 'let go of', not suppressed or avoided but just mindfully observed (Kabatt-Zinn 2004). Other types of meditation such as transcendental meditation (TM) use similar approaches in which a word or mantra is brought to mind in a state of relaxation, the attention is focussed inwards, and this is done for a period of 20 minutes twice daily. Thoughts are allowed to drift into the mind but the attention will return to the mantra. This author's experience is with TM and he has found it useful from a personal perspective and useful with patients. With patients who are very busy and active it is a way of getting them to slow down and relax, and also to reduce muscle tension. In terms of the research there has been a recent exploratory study with CFS patients suggesting that meditation could have an effect on fatigue, mood, quality of life and physical function, though further research is required (Surawy, Roberts and Silver 2005). A meta-analysis of meditation used with a wide range of problems found an effect size of 0.5, although there were only a few acceptable studies (Grossman, Niemann, Schmidt and Wallach 2004).

A meditation programme for CFS

This can be taught to the patient, or the handout below can be given. It is important to discuss with the patient the potential helpfulness of this approach.

Meditation is an approach that has been used for centuries, for spiritual and religious reasons, and also more recently for the relief of pain and stress. We have found that meditation can ease the symptoms of CFS, and we would ask you to practise this on a regular basis in order to get the most benefit. Our experience with this meditation is that the more one practises it the better it gets. What happens in this meditation is that you turn your attention inwards on to a word or 'mantra', and in this case we will use the word 'peace' though you can use any word of your choice or a sound like 'om'. When you do this you will find your body relaxing, and your breathing and heart rate slowing. Let's now do the meditation.

Make sure as much as possible that other people will not disturb you when you do the meditation. The same applies to telephones and general noise, though it may be impossible to totally escape these. Also do not take a lot of caffeine drinks before the meditative practice, as it will interfere with the process.

Get comfortable on your chair; you do not have to sit completely still. The important thing is to be comfortable. Sit with you eyes closed for two minutes (again you do not have to sit with your eyes closed, but this aids the meditation). Wear a watch so you can check your time, as your sense of time may become distorted. Start saying the word 'peace' out loud, pausing for about five seconds between each time you say it. Then slowly get quieter and quieter, and then just say the word 'peace' in your mind. Do this for 15–20 minutes and then stop, sit with your eyes closed again for two minutes and then open them. If you find that your thoughts are drifting away from the word on to other concerns, then gently direct them back to it.

The role of the clinician who is teaching meditation

Take the patient through this and ask how they found the process. Most patients feel 'relaxed', 'heavy', and that their breathing was slow. Ask the patient before and afterwards whether they have any questions or comments: clinical experience is that most people are willing to try it. Occasionally some patients feel a bit strange and out of control particularly if it has been a powerful experience and they are person for whom control is very important. One can reassure them that they are not out of control and that practising themselves will allow them to be in control and obtain benefits, including being more relaxed and hopefully having reduced pain (and possibly fatigue). The experience is that some patients get some benefit and others do not. The main mechanisms are likely to be: getting the person to slow down and make time for themselves, physical and mental relaxation, and detaching from distressing thoughts by the attention paid to the mantra. It is probably better not to provide such a rationalistic explanation but to ask the patient just to experience it. The patient should be asked to commit to practising it once or twice a day and possibly also if their symptoms were severe, or they were feeling particularly stressed. It is important to evaluate how patients are getting on with it. Some patients have difficulty 'fitting it in', so one can try to problem solve this with them. Some people have used it to try to get to sleep and found it to work well. If it is working for the patient then encourage them to use it, but if not then one needs to move on to other strategies.

If the patient does not like the idea of meditation then one could use an imagery approach. One would ask the patient to sit with their eyes closed for two minutes and then ask them to visualise their favourite scene such as a beach or a garden. One would ask them to slowly go through each of the five senses of sight, smell, hearing, touch and taste, spending quite a few minutes vividly imaging each sense, and becoming fully aware of the scene. The patient could also take themselves on a walk through the scene, for example walking down the steps to the garden. Again one would hope that they would feel relaxed and the pain would reduce. The clinician should discuss the importance of everyday practice. The whole area of meditation is a large one. If the clinician or patient wishes to develop the approaches further then a good place to start is Kabatt-Zinn's 'Full Catastrophe Living' (2004).

It is helpful to emphasise that there are a variety of relaxation techniques, and if the patient wishes to use a specific one that they prefer, then this is fine.

Poor concentration and other neuropsychological complaints

These types of complaints occur in 85 per cent of patients with CFS (Grafman 1994). Common complaints range from forgetfulness, distractibility, decreased concentration and impaired reasoning ability (Tiersky, Johnson, Lange, Natelson and DeLuca 1997), with patients who have depression alongside CFS having the most complaints (Cope et al 1996). Tiersky et al (1997) conducted a comprehensive review of the literature and concluded that intellectual function is normal and, regarding the area of attention/memory, that patients perform normally with simple tests but at a lower capacity with more complex material. In terms of learning and memory there is no deficit in the recall of memories from long term storage but there is some evidence of decreased initial acquisition. Patients with CFS may have more difficulty learning and recalling complex verbal material but higher order skills of concept formation/reasoning, etc., are intact. It is not possible to explain these deficits because of depression. The subjective complaints of patients are generally greater than those found on objective neuropsychological testing, and this is unexplained (Tiersky et al 1997).

Useful suggestions to help patients who have these problems would be to:

- Treat any mood disturbances such as depression by psychological or medication approaches. Explain that there is evidence that mood problems can make attention/memory problems worse.
- Reassure the patient that intellectual function is not damaged. Reassure them that long term memory is intact but they may have some problems with short term memory.
- Ask the patient to consider avoiding complex material. If they must work with complex material then the following principles are important: they may have to work harder to remember things by rehearsal of the material in their minds; by reading something more often than normal; by making more notes; by using memory prompts such as flashcards and material put into mobile phones and electronic and paper organisers. They should break down a learning task into manageable chunks and should take short breaks afterwards (Meier, Benton and Diller 1987). It may be that the standard way of associating things with powerful or meaningful imagery would help their memories (Meier, Benton and Diller 1987).
- Understand that patients are often very hard on themselves, saying 'I used to be able to do this so easily and I'm so pathetic at it now', and here it is important to help patients understand that they are ill and cannot be expected to perform, for the time being, at previous levels.
- Explain that cognitive problems should improve as the CFS improves.

Gastrointestinal disturbances and irritable bowel

There is an increased incidence of gastrointestinal problems in CFS sufferers (86 per cent), compared to controls (56 per cent), reported in Burnet and Chatterton (2001). Irritable bowel syndrome (IBS), which is characterised by bloating, abdominal pain and constipation/diarrhoea, is also commonly diagnosed in CFS (Van Konynenburg 2003). The causes of IBS are debated, but it is possible that some of the factors (predisposing, precipitating and maintenance) described earlier could be important. If one can successfully work with these factors then it is possible that the IBS symptoms will reduce. It is also possible that CBT for CFS could be modified to particularly try to help IBS symptoms.

In terms of the evidence base for the treatment of IBS, a Cochrane review (Evans, Clark, Moore and Whorell 2005), looking at the newer drug Tegaserod, concluded that current drug treatments were of limited value. Tegaserod did have an impact on the global symptoms of IBS, pain and discomfort in non-constipated females with IBS but there was inadequate information about men. Lackner, Mesmer, Morley, Dowzer and Hamilton (2004) in a meta-analysis of psychological treatments found that they were better than controls. One RCT shows CBT to be more effective than an education group in 'functional bowel disorders' (Burnett and Drossman 2004). The role of diet in the treatment of IBS is less clear: high fibre diets have been used but their effectiveness is uncertain (Talley and Spiller 2002).

Principles of CBT in IBS

As before with the main symptoms of CFS, the clinician would be trying to develop a formulation looking at potential maintenance factors for these IBS symptoms. This would be looking at emotional, environmental, cognitive, physical and behavioural factors. It is always worth getting the patient to keep a diary, identifying frequency of symptoms, triggering factors and responses. When one successfully identifies these and develops a mini-formulation then the next stage is to use the CBT approaches described in this book to modify them. This may be used in conjunction with diet, medication and other approaches (Darnley and Millar 2003):

- Stage 1: assess the problem and develop a formulation.
- Stage 2: provide information about IBS, such as: one bout of symptoms can make us vulnerable to another bout, IBS is a problem of the way the bowel functions, it is unlikely to get worse and will probably come and go, it is difficult to be sure about the prognosis, and the symptoms, although they are unpleasant, cannot harm the body. It is possible to modify cognitive, behavioural, stress and lifestyle factors that contribute to it (Darnley and Millar 2003; Toner, Segal, Emmott and Myran 2000).
- Stage 3: help the patient with behavioural change. These changes depend on what has been found at the assessment, and may include bad toilet habits such as: having to go to the toilet at a set time; being unable to leave the house until the bowels have been moved; holding on excessively for fear of causing smells or making embarrassing noises through wind or defecation; restricting eating (times/types of foods/places) for fear of worsening symptoms; refusing to go anywhere unless there is immediate access to a toilet; straining hard to move the bowels; excessive monitoring of the shape, size and consistency of the stool; spending excessive time on the toilet or going to the toilet at the first sign of abdominal discomfort. Examples of behavioural change statements may be: I will not spend more than ten minutes on the toilet; I will ensure that I have my breakfast each morning; I will not carry pads about with me in case I have an accident. As before these behavioural changes need to have clear rationale and a regular process of review.
- Stage 4: tackle cognitive distortions. Some of the negative thoughts and beliefs that are found in IBS are 'I have a serious illness, like cancer', 'I'm likely to have an accident if I don't get to the toilet straight away', 'It's awful if anyone notices me breaking wind', 'If I don't go to the toilet each day, I'm bound to get constipated'. Underlying rules and beliefs may be around themes of control, perfectionism, other people's opinions and worry (Toner et al 2000), though this has not been systematically investigated. Patients may also, if they become stuck in an emotional state like anxiety, excessively switch their attention to their symptoms, leading to an amplification of these symptoms.

- Stage 5: consider teaching the patient meditation/relaxation if there is an excessive degree of anxious arousal.
- Stage 6: address environmental factors. If the person is in a stressful job, in an unhappy relationship, has money worries, etc., then it may be possible to help the person with these, possibly using a problem solving approach.
- Stage 7: consider the person's diet. Ensure at the least that they are eating regularly and sensibly with a good balance of nutrients and that they are drinking two litres of water a day.
- Stage 8: ensure that they are taking adequate exercise, but consider this also in light of their CFS symptoms.
- Stage 9: review medication if you are qualified to do this, and if not ask that they do this with their GP.
- Stage 10: review whether gender issues are important, and discuss them with the patient. Possible areas here are whether women are more likely than men to be non-assertive, self-sacrificing and suppressive of anger, and whether this has any impact on the symptoms (Toner et al 2000).

See Darnley and Millar for further information about IBS.

Impact of symptoms on activities of daily living

The consideration of the tremendous impact that the symptoms and experience of CFS can have on the person's ability to live their life is not a subject that is much written about in the CFS literature, but it is one that is very important for the patient. Examples are:

- Functioning at a poor level at *work*, because of fatigue and poor concentration; the design of the workplace being poor for the person's changed circumstances; the hours that the person has been working being difficult to sustain; risk of the person being dismissed from their job.
- Being unable to do normal *domestic tasks* such as getting dressed and self-caring; having difficulty looking after children, doing housework, going shopping, gardening; these may be a particular problem for women.
- Being unable to enjoy a *sex life* because of pain and fatigue.
- Not being able to take moderate amounts of *alcohol*. Most patients describe intolerance to alcohol, and for some patients the enjoyment and stress relieving elements of drinking are missed.
- *Heat, cold and noise sensitivity.*
- Finding it difficult to *drive* because of pain from turning the steering wheel.
- Having to interact with the *benefits or insurance system.*
- Struggling to pursue old *hobbies and interests*, particularly if these have been quite active.
- Having to live with *pain, fatigue and uncertainty.*

In talking about these issues we are skirting between the issues of helping the person with the problem but also adjusting to the reality of the symptoms. Often the question of how long the symptoms will continue is asked, and one is put in the position of trying to be positive and helping the person engage with constructive therapies, but not being unrealistically optimistic, if faced with challenging problems. There are also the issues of what the research says about longer term follow up of CBT of CFS; the only paper the author is aware of is Deale et al (2001), and the patient can be quoted the results of this. The author's practice is to say, 'It is unlikely that things will change quickly, so you should be prepared for this. In my experience of seeing patients in a specialist clinic some do well and get rid of all of their symptoms, but the biggest group in the middle make different degrees of progress, particularly with functioning well and improved mood, and also with reduction in symptoms. A minority of patients do not seem to make any progress at all. (The Deale et al study, which looked at five year follow-up, suggested that 68 per cent of patients rated themselves as 'improved' or 'very improved'. However many patients had remaining symptoms.)'

This author's attempt to deal with some of these factors is described below.

Work

This area is of fundamental importance for patients with CFS. In terms of precipitating and maintenance factors it is often the stress of work that contributes to their symptoms. When the symptoms are severe it is difficult to manage the workload. At a public health level there may be something to be done to reduce the overwork culture that seems to be increasing in the Western world in recent years: indeed if CFS is increasing this may be one of the issues implicated. Useful things that could be done at a public health level may be a limit on long hours, provision of exercise facilities, ensuring that adequate rests and holidays are taken, discouragement from taking work home, and so on. Changes like this need to be balanced against business's need for profitability and competitiveness. In terms of the person's ability to do their job, one can start with the usual principles about pacing, taking all breaks, finishing on time, and so on. Often one is in a position to support this with medical evidence about their diagnosis, and the importance of excessive demands not being put on them: one does have to be careful, however, that one does not paint such a gloomy picture that the employer wants to dismiss the person. Employers vary in their responsiveness, but most recognise their legal and moral responsibility to look after their staff, and probably bigger organisations are in a better position to do this than small companies. If one is not in a position to provide evidence oneself about the patient's condition, then the GP may be helped to do so. It is also wise to provide evidence after discussing the matter carefully with the GP and it can also help to get their occupational health service involved.

A letter the author wrote recently on behalf of a patient, who was working in a call centre providing computer support, was as follows:

Dear Sir,

Thank you for your recent letter asking for a report on Mr. Smith. I can confirm that he does meet the diagnostic criteria for Chronic Fatigue Syndrome. This is a condition characterised in Mr. Smith's case by extreme fatigue, widespread muscle pain, and dizziness. You will be aware that he has only had four weeks off sick in the last year, despite significant symptoms, and I am quite clear that he is motivated to attend work and do his job to his normal level. In terms of your question about how his work can be modified to help his performance we would suggest that the amount of time he spends in actual calls is reduced, we would suggest by 20%, and his work on e-mail support increased by 20%. We would also suggest that he is allowed to take his three rest breaks a day, as sometimes this has not been happening. We would hope that this change would allow him to perform well and have less fatigue symptoms. He is as ever appreciative of the support you have given him up to now.

Yours faithfully
Philip Kinsella

If employers are unreasonable or unco-operative then the letter may have to be framed in a more insistent or persuasive way, though obviously one has to tread warily. Employers are aware that workers have obtained compensation because their employees have not been protected from undue stress, and possibly this fact can be used in the negotiation.

Regarding the issue of taking time off work, one encounters a variety of responses: some patients take appropriate time off; others, often because of their perfectionism, push themselves to go to work when they should probably be off, and these patients often say 'I've got too much to do', 'I'm the only person who can do it', and so on. Other patients who are perhaps more anxious may take frequent or indeed what seems an excessive amount of time off; often the patients who do this really do not like their jobs or are frightened that the job will make them worse if they go back to it. The therapist is making some degree of subjective judgement around this. The best approach is to raise the issue with the patient and try to work it through together, perhaps writing down the pros and cons of being at work. Similarly with the issue of working hours, it may be possible to help the patient reduce their working hours to a level that they are better able to manage the numerous demands on them. One wants to adopt a balance between helping the patient balance demands whilst maintaining a rehabilitative focus on the importance of working.

Sometimes the patient's job is under threat. The circumstances can range from a situation where the patient is relieved that they will be made redundant, to a situation in which job loss would be fairly disastrous for the person and their family. Often this is because the person is not 'performing well', and often this puts the patient in a difficult position because trying to meet the demands of the job could potentially worsen symptoms, whereas not doing so could increase the likelihood of dismissal. One can again try to help the person negotiate alterations in their job plan that strike a balance. One can also work specifically in dealing with how the person's dysfunctional assumptions around perfectionism and achievement are being activated in the work environment (if this is the case). They may need to learn to delegate tasks, not do all work to the same standard, refuse tasks, and not take work home. If the person's job is in real danger then they should take advice from their union or solicitor.

Occasionally it is clear from assessment that work is a very significant factor in the maintenance of the symptoms, and there is a dilemma about whether the job should be resigned from or whether another career can be pursued. A problem solving approach is worth using here and indeed in other situations where patients have stuck points and dilemmas (Hawton et al 1989: Chapter 12).

Problem solving

This strategy involves addressing difficult and stressful situations in order to change them. It may be particularly helpful to use problem solving in the following situations:

- The person is in dilemma or is facing a difficult life choice
- The person has a number of 'real life' problems or crises, which could include dealing with a physical illness, a financial crisis, having to move home or dealing with a deteriorating personal relationship

Whether one should adopt a more standard CBT approach or use problem solving may depend on whether the person was thinking about the situation in a dysfunctional way. If they were generally not, then a problem solving approach may be helpful; indeed the crisis may be leading to so many disturbances that standard CBT is difficult.

There is evidence that this approach can be used effectively as a sole therapy with depression, and indeed helping cancer patients to cope (D'Zurilla and Nezu 2000). If it is used, then there is a well-established protocol (Neenan and Dryden 2002):

1   *Problem identification.* It is important here to define the problem in precise language, e.g. 'I am likely to be made redundant in March which will lead to a 75 per cent reduction of my income'.
2   *Goal selection.* Again the person should express this clearly and in a way that is measurable.
3   *Generation of alternatives.* This step is to generate as many possible solutions as possible, even if they are highly unlikely (often called 'brainstorming'). Sometimes the therapist needs to prompt the person to get them started.

4 *Consideration of consequences.* The next stage is to consider the advantages and disadvantages of each alternative. If one wanted to elaborate then one could consider this in the short and long term and even the consequences for significant other people.

5 *Decision making.* Here the person is asked to consider the alternatives that most likely help them reach their goals. There may be one or more. This is probably the most difficult stage, as one can be faced with several possibilities that look equally attractive, or more often unattractive. It may help to give a numerical value to each alternative on a scale of 1–10. This could measure 'usefulness' or 'desirableness'. It is probably necessary at this stage to have quite a prolonged discussion with the patient and they are likely to require time to think about it and discuss it with friends/family. It is important that one does not impose one's preferred solution onto the patient, though this can be tempting.

6 *Implementation.* If the person has made up their mind then the next stage is to put it into practice. Depending on the task, this may be difficult. As before, role-play, grading and discussion of the consequences are the things to do.

7 *Evaluation.* Did the implementing of the solution achieve the goal, or move towards the goal? If it did not it may be that the person has implemented the solution inadequately or without persistence, or they are lacking in the necessary skills to do so. It may also be that there are real life obstacles to achieving it. Depending on the cause of the failure one might work with further coaching in the skills to help achieve the solution or the person may have to return to considering rejected alternatives. Some problems may just not have a solution, and one can just try to help the person cope with a very distressing circumstance (Sharoff 2002).

Domestic tasks

Patients because of their symptoms can find different degrees of difficulty in dong these tasks. Some severely affected patients feel unable to do basic self-care activities like bathing, cooking, and dressing. Some have become bed bound. Most patients feel worse after they do household tasks.

The bed bound patient is a particular challenge. Detailed assessment of the reasons why they are in this situation needs to be made, and particular attention should be given to psychiatric disorder, disadvantages of getting better and iatrogenic factors. Often the patients have become quite deconditioned and dependent and are worried about getting severe pain from small activities. One can only work with such patients from a multidisciplinary approach, probably with the family and certainly with the GP, physiotherapy and occupational health colleagues. The treatment process is no different with the emphasis on a detailed assessment of maintenance factors, and an attempt to motivate and rehabilitate the patient through small activity steps. These may include sitting out of bed for short periods, doing gentle exercises like stretching in bed, and reading self-help material. There is a lack of literature on programmes for these very disabled people, but plainly such approaches will take up a lot of clinical time and be conducted in the person's home.

Aside from the bed bound patient, most sufferers describe feeling significantly more pain and fatigue from doing tasks like cleaning. The principle of pacing is probably most helpful here. Some patients, particularly women, seem very driven to push on and do housework beyond a reasonable level. This may be linked into a sense of their identity being formed by their ability to look after the house, or it may be part of a general perfectionism. Sometimes a dynamic develops in the household in that the female partner has for years taken on considerable household responsibilities, and the other members of the families have been left with few. If the patient is struggling now to meet those responsibilities there is a task to help them delegate work or persuade their family to take on more responsibilities. Regarding childcare, again this can be primarily a woman's responsibility and one that can be difficult to fulfil if they are ill. Interestingly this author has met a few patients whose symptoms have diminished when they have become pregnant and had children. Sometimes it can feel like the symptoms exist to allow the woman to have a break from intolerable domestic pressures.

Obviously the therapist's role is to identify these patterns and help the patient reduce excessive household demands by:

- Getting their partners to do more
- Getting children to do more
- Enlisting family help
- Enlisting paid domestic help
- Trying to gain assistance from the benefit system to pay for help

Again one is striking a balance between reducing demands and having a rehabilitative focus. Often the behavioural change plan involves reducing household tasks and increasing exercise activities. For example:

1   I will delegate the daily task of vacuuming and sweeping the floor to my husband (as agreed with him).
2   Every second day I will go to the baths by myself and have two 15-minute swimming sessions.

Sex life

If one asks, many patients will describe problems with their sex lives. The usual difficulties are that they do not have the energy to have sex, or that because of the pain they have sex is indeed painful. There is no clear solution to this problem. Obviously one would hope that as their fatigue and pain improved then their sex life would too. They may need to reduce the frequency of sex, but put more emphasis on quality! Sometimes if patients are on SSRI anti-depressants then loss of libido and ability to have an erection is a problem. If muscle pain is a problem then commonsense advice can be given about being slow and gentle. There is information in the pain self-help book 'Overcoming Chronic Pain' by Cole, MacDonald, Carus and Howden Leach (2005) as to what may be the most comfortable positions.

Alcohol sensitivity

Almost all patients will describe this if asked about it, usually saying that they are more affected or intoxicated than before or that alcohol makes them feel unwell. This is a puzzling and interesting aspect of CFS physiology, and it is difficult to think of what can be done from a CBT perspective. Because they are sensitive most patients will not drink alcohol, and obviously one would not suggest they do so. If a patient has been dependent on alcohol to relax then extra effort has to be put in to find alternative ways to unwind.

Heat, cold and noise sensitivity

Again this is very common and unpleasant. Patients will describe either being too hot in the summer and extra cold in the winter. Many find normal noises unpleasant and intolerable. Again it is difficult to think what to do, and this is another strange feature of the physiology of CFS: one could measure the person's temperature to see if there are objective abnormalities. The person may need to drink more, wear extra light clothes in the summer and wear extra heavy clothes in the winter.

Driving

Patients with CFS are often keen to continue to drive (because of difficulty walking), but often find that doing so leads to worsening symptoms. Repeated turning of the steering wheel seems to be a common trigger. Apart from the usual advice about pacing and taking short journeys, it is difficult to think of a strategy to help this. Some patients become frightened to drive because they feel that their processing of information in terms of concentration and attention is impaired. Also some patients who sleep poorly and are inclined to fall asleep through the day may be more likely to fall asleep at the wheel. The clinician's task is to help the person objectively assess their ability to drive, and this may be aided by sitting with them in the car. Another suggestion may be advanced driving lessons.

The benefits and insurance situation

When people are ill they may be entitled to state benefits and insurance and plainly this entitlement will vary depending on the person's circumstances. It is perfectly reasonable for CFS patients to get the benefits they are entitled to, and it is correct to support the person in their claim. However there is also evidence that patients who are involved in benefits claims have 'significantly poorer outcomes' (Prins, Bleijenberg, Bazelmans, Elving, de Boo, Severens, van der Wilt, Spinhoven and van der Meer 2002), and one would not wish the patient to get into a benefit trap if it was going to block their recovery from the condition. This author's experience is that even if patients do get insurance/benefits then they are usually still keen to recover from the condition. Clinicians are often asked by patients to support them with their claims, and it can be hard to refuse this even if one is dubious about the helpfulness of the claim. Time limited benefits are often helpful in that they give the patient a target to get better for. Another problem in doing a report is that one is often asked about prognosis. As stated earlier, if the person is having a course of CBT then one can quote the five year follow-up study (Deale et al 2001) described earlier, and relate that to your individual patient.

Hobbies and interests

It is important for CFS patients to participate in meaningful hobbies and interests. Often the ones they did before are harder to engage with because of symptoms, and a task may be to find alternatives with the patient. This can be a particular problem for the patient who has engaged in a lot of vigorous sports activities that are now difficult to do. Often these activities were successful as 'stressbusters', and the loss of them may be a maintenance factor. Also patients' mood may dip if the previously important hobbies are unavailable to them. Days can be very long for those suffering significant symptoms. It is also important that patients are encouraged to visit friends and family and draw support from them. (This is if they are supportive: many patients say that their families do not understand them because they don't 'look ill', and friends can sometimes be less keen to spend time with a person who gets tired very easily and is less able to pursue joint interests.)

Living with ongoing pain, fatigue and uncertainty

In CBT work with CFS sufferers one is negotiating between working actively to get people better in terms of meeting targets for mood, symptoms and functioning, and helping them adjust to the disability that they have. The initial assessment is important in determining how one thinks the patient will do, and how successful one can be at bringing about improvements. In reality many patients will be left with symptoms (Deale et al 2001), and work may have to shift from treatment to adjustment. This author's approach is to try to treat the patient if it is possible to identify credible maintenance factors, and also to be realistic about outcomes in order not to set the patient up with unrealistic expectations.

Adjustment and rehabilitation

In this stage of intervention, which may be conducted alongside more active treatment or if this was significantly unsuccessful, the person is being helped 'to manage physical restrictions that limit their activities or functioning' (Uslan 2003). The family needs to be involved and needs to be supported. It may be difficult to live with someone who has a chronic condition and the relative may be feeling stressed and exhausted. Sometimes they need to be directed to specialist carer networks and support groups, and sometimes the therapist can get them practical help from the benefits system. How much the CBT clinician gets involved with the family will depend on the dynamic between the patient, their family and the therapist's role.

The patient may experience grief, for the loss of their own role, their health and their dreams and aspirations. From a CBT perspective the person may have difficulty accepting that symptoms are not going to clear up, and there may be some avoidance of considering this. This can be problematic if the therapist has been upbeat about improvement and this has not occurred, and it can be tempting for the clinician to collude in an over-optimistic approach. This is compounded by the fact that outcome in CFS can be difficult to judge and some patients seem to get better of their own accord after a discouraging course. If the clinician thinks that the outlook is not good because of an adequate trial of all evidence based treatments that has no response (and this can happen), then they need to be indicating that the person must adjust to the symptoms that are likely to be there for a long time. The things that they need to focus on are:

* Gaining and maintaining the support of their GP
* Ensuring medication use is effective
* Gaining help in adjusting lifestyle, e.g., making practical changes to the house and car, which make them easier to use. The occupational therapist may be able to advise on this
* Eating well, exercising and maintaining general health
* Using electronic aides such as 'Personal Digital Assistants' to aid memory and concentration problems
* Getting the best out of support groups and advocacy groups
* Getting the most out of being in the disabled category, e.g. travelling provisions, work rehabilitation, 'expert patient program'
* Getting the most out of alternative medicine approaches

(See Uslan et al 2003.)

Relapse prevention

If your treatment has been more successful and there has been a reduction in symptoms and/or an increase in functioning and mood, then it is important to have a relapse prevention section towards the end of therapy. (This is not an ideal phrase as it was developed for more 'treatable' conditions such as phobias: a more helpful phrase may be 'maintaining progress'.) One has to make a decision with the patient when to discharge them into the process of follow-up, and this is usually done when the person is showing signs of reasonable progress toward their goals, and measurable improvements on measures of mood or functioning or symptoms can be shown. The idea is that one is confident that the patient can apply the CBT approach by themselves and is willing to do so. Then follow-up appointments, usually for a year, are arranged at between intervals of two to six months. Again this is not a perfect model because we are dealing with conditions that may persist at some level for a long time, and a model of ongoing care or easy access back into the service is probably preferable.

The process of relapse prevention involves the person filling in a form that analyses and summarises what has been helpful to the patient, what may cause relapses and setbacks, and how progress can be maintained and problems dealt with. A number of patients do not get to this stage, as they will drop out before it is reached. An example of such a form is given in Figure 7.1.

One would hope that in the first section the patient would talk about the strategies that one has used with them: this may include behavioural strategies, problem solving, sleep management, etc. They may mention things that are not directly related to CBT, such as family support and medication. In terms of what can cause relapse, then things that are often mentioned are physical illness, stressful life events and excessive demands. In the final section one has the opportunity to help the person continue with the programme and fit it more naturally into their lifestyle. One should emphasise with the person that lapses and setbacks are normal and that does not mean the person is slipping back to square one. One should also warn about the importance of remaining focussed on CBT even if they are not in regular contact with a therapist. It can help to suggest that the patient has a CBT session 'with themselves' once a month, to more formally go over their progress, therapy strategies and goals, and their partner can be involved in this.

Sometimes as patients get better they revert to the old lifestyle:

Patient example: Angela had made good progress in reducing the excessive demands that were on her from work, and the demands of the home. She had also reduced the tendency to eat junk food, and had been losing the weight that she had put on. As a consequence of this and regular swimming sessions her fatigue had almost disappeared. It was disappointing to see at three month follow-up that she had thrown herself back into her old lifestyle after her daughter become ill for a period; she had suffered a lapse and a significant increase in symptoms. The follow-up session was focussed on getting her back on track and learning from the experience.

RELAPSE PREVENTION

This form is intended to be a blueprint that you can develop with your therapist in order to maintain and build on progress. Please answer these questions.

What has helped you?

What could cause problems in the future?

What do you need to do to deal with these problems and generally maintain progress?

Figure 7.1   Relapse prevention form.

Chapter summary

Cognitive behavioural therapy may have a role to play with other problems that occur in CFS. Pain is common, and CBT can be one strategy used. There is some evidence that meditation may be helpful in CFS, and a transcendental meditation exercise is described. Patients also have problems with attention and memory, but there is no damage to long term memory or intellectual function: the therapist can reassure the patient, treat mood disturbances and suggest specific CBT approaches. Irritable bowel syndrome is more common in CFS, and CBT could be one approach used to address stress, diet and unhelpful thinking and behavioural patterns. The symptoms themselves can have a major impact on the person's ability to fulfil their activities of daily living such as work, and this becomes harder if the person does not improve much and has to be helped to adjust to the remaining disability. The CBT role therefore is to help the patient ensure that they have adequate skills to maintain progress or adjust to disability.

Chapter 8

Catherine's story

In this chapter a patient will give her account of the lead up to her CFS illness, her experience of the condition, and her view of CBT. This will be interspersed by my commentary, which will describe the course of treatment, including the difficulties and dilemmas encountered. Catherine's story begins:

> I was in my fifties and, apart from the usual annual cold, the odd 'tummy bug' and a couple of bouts of proper flu some thirty years ago, I had hardly ever been ill in my life. I lived alone as my partner had died 15 years ago and my children had married and left home. I was working full time in a busy middle management job, doing all the household chores and tending a large garden without any trouble or any outside help. I was physically fit, exercised regularly and clocked up over 1000 miles a year cycling to and from work.
>
> That summer I started my three-week break from work doing some much needed decorating at home and I began to feel unusually tired. I told myself this was to be expected, I was not as young as I used to be and had been working very hard lately; so I just got on with the decorating knowing that I would be glad when it was done. As I stood back to admire my efforts I felt very, very tired. This was not a normal, almost pleasant, tiredness but complete exhaustion.

(It is common for patients to differentiate between the normal tiredness that can occur and the fatigue of the condition.)

> I decided to rest and regain my normal energy, but this did not happen. Instead of feeling refreshed and energetic I began to feel ill.

(Patients often try to manage their tiredness by rest but this may not work.)

A sore throat appeared along with a headache, aching muscles and a feverish feeling. I told myself that it must be a summer cold coming. But the illness did not develop into a cold, it persisted just as it was and I began to suffer from a wheezy cough every time I lay down. This kept me awake at night and I finally visited my GP where a diagnosis of 'chest infection' was made. I was prescribed antibiotics, my holiday ended and I returned to work feeling disappointed, unrefreshed and less than well.

Over the next two months I failed to get any better and two more bottles of antibiotics were prescribed, with no effect. I began to feel more and more ill and found that the effort of cycling to work was starting to sap my energy. So I finally did something that I had never done before; I allowed myself a 'self certificate' week off work and rested for much of the time.

(Some patients never allow themselves to have time off work.)

This did make me feel a lot better and I returned to work expecting to feel properly well within a few days.

Sadly, after two days back at my desk I felt worse than ever and I started to worry that there might be something seriously wrong. To get to the staff toilets I had to climb a flight of stairs. I used to be able to run up the stairs but all of a sudden my legs felt like stone and I had a real struggle to visit the toilet. I decided to go back to see the doctor where various blood tests were taken, but they all came back 'normal'. Finally I was sent for a chest x-ray and then told that I had adult onset asthma. I was prescribed steroid tablets and inhalers, patted on the back, and told it would settle down in time.

For the next three months I forced myself to carry on normally even though I felt exhausted and ill.

(This can be a typical coping pattern.)

I told myself that lots of people cope with asthma and I was just being silly. I took the steroid tablets as instructed and the cough went away but the awful flu like feeling was still there and I began to suffer from drenching night sweats, abdominal bloating and troubled sleep. I also had pain in my torso, shoulders and arms. There were tender spots that, if touched, felt as though they were bruised or stung [like wasp stings].

Back at work in the New Year I had a little more energy and decided to take myself in hand. I spent a small fortune on vitamin and mineral supplements and started exercising two or three evenings a week to try and get fitter. It was then that I noticed that my muscles hurt during the exercises as well as afterwards. I used to enjoy exercising but it had become painful and my energy was so low that I had to push myself very hard.

(It can be difficult to judge what the correct level of exercise is.)

After about a week of my new regime I began to feel awful again, but I hid how I felt from my work colleagues and denied it even to myself. This went on for some weeks and then one day I was sitting at my desk and the telephone rang but I hadn't the energy to answer it. Instead I started to cry and my boss told me to go home. It was such a relief to get home and lay down. I told myself that tomorrow is another day and I would feel better.

However, instead of feeling any better I started to feel so poorly that I was unable to go to work for a whole week at a time. There seemed to be a sort of pattern to the illness. I felt more or less normal after resting for a couple of days, went back to work, got tired and then spent the next few days feeling extremely ill. In fact I had never felt so ill before in my life. There were many times when the effort of making myself a hot drink used all my energy and I was forced to lay and watch the drink go cold, not having the energy to pick the cup up and drink it. A new doctor cut the steroids out very gradually and, as this happened, I realised that they had been masking what was now a serious infection. I had an excruciatingly sore ulcerated mouth and throat and a hideous widespread rash that developed into blisters that were two inches across in places. The GP did some blood tests that were normal.

By now it was spring and my previously booked holiday in Majorca was a few days away. My legs felt like two blocks of concrete hanging from my hips, my arms felt so heavy that I couldn't move them and I collapsed on to my bed and cried bitterly. There was no way that I could go away feeling like this. My holiday had to be cancelled and I spent the Easter break resting in bed and trying to keep cheerful.

Over the next few months my GP referred me to three different specialists, without anything being found.

I decided to put all my limited energy into my job, as concern had been raised about my attendance. Sadly my memory began to fail me and I had to keep a secret 'diary' of every conversation and telephone call. At the same time my thinking, which used to be crystal clear, became 'muzzy'. Work started to pile up as my decision-making skills deteriorated and problems that I once solved easily now appeared exhausting and insurmountable. I also started to feel faint quite frequently; my body was telling me something but I was not listening. I was not the sort of person who got ill; this was a total nightmare.

Then one day I felt much better. I had a burst of energy similar to that experienced by a woman just before going into labour. I went shopping on my way home from work but half way home I suddenly felt faint while riding my bike and I fell off and collapsed in a heap at the side of the road. My shopping rolled down the hill behind me never to be seen again. A passer by took me to the doctor's surgery where my injuries were treated. Fortunately I was not badly hurt, just minor cuts and bruises, so I was driven home and told to see my GP next day. I was seriously shaken by my collapse and determined not to have a repeat performance, so in the morning I telephoned my boss and told him that I would not be back until I was better. I never returned to work.

After examining me yet again my GP referred me to a Rheumatologist who examined me and I winced when he pressed on my painful areas. Then I sat by his desk and he looked at me over his glasses. 'You have got Chronic Fatigue Syndrome' he said. I was relieved to have a name for my illness but I had never heard of the condition so I asked him to listen to my list of symptoms again so as to be quite sure.

The Consultant sat and nodded as I listed my malaise, overwhelming fatigue, feverish feelings, migraine headaches, permanent sore throat, muscle aches, painful areas on my body, poor sleep, muzzy headedness, fainting attacks, poor balance, abdominal pain, bloating, coughing, wheezing, skin rashes, night sweats and inappropriate daytime sweating. I asked him how many of these symptoms could possibly be part of this one illness. He paused and then said 'All of them'. I had waited for this diagnosis for nineteen months and I felt reassured until I asked what the treatment was. He said 'There isn't any specific treatment but I will refer you on to Clinical Psychology to see if something like Cognitive Behavioural Therapy might help'. I was in a daze. An illness without a cure? Referral for a psychological treatment? He must think this is all in my mind.

(Again, this reaction is common.)

I only just made it outside the hospital before the tears began to fall. I felt humiliated, worried, confused and, above all, just plain ill. I wanted to wake up and find it had all been a nightmare.

I was concerned that my work colleagues didn't seem to understand how a previously energetic person had become a virtual cabbage and one by one they stopped contacting me. Presumably they didn't know what to say to me. Only my true friends were left, but I didn't have the energy to visit them or even talk to them on the phone for more than about ten minutes at a time.

While I was still waiting for my CBT assessment appointment I had a letter from my employers with the news I had been dreading. My job could only be held open for me for a total of one year. I felt desperate that I should get treated and get back to work.

Catherine was referred by the consultant rheumatologist to my clinic in the General Hospital Department of Psychological Medicine. On assessment her main problem was severe fatigue, which was present 80 per cent of the time. She also described muscle aches, mental tiredness, headaches, sore throats, cough and wheeze and other symptoms, as described above. Physical things such as shopping, walking and seeing her grandchildren worsened the problem. Her behavioural response in the past was to push herself on. She said it was difficult to balance her life because she was a busy person. She described the onset and history of the problem as detailed above. She described a somewhat difficult early experience in that her father was strict, authoritarian and 'old school', but otherwise her upbringing was good. She possibly under-achieved academically, but got a job in an architect's office and then worked as a business manager in a company. A very significant event was having a longstanding relationship with a man who was married. She had a son and a daughter with this man who was called Paul. Unfortunately Paul died in very difficult circumstances, and she had to bring up her children by herself.

I developed a tentative formulation and agreed that she suffered from chronic fatigue syndrome; I thought that one could see how some of her symptoms can be explained in psychological terms, namely her early experience of her dad being strict, and the rules that arise from this could be predisposing factors; we were able to identify unhelpful rules such as 'I should put others first', 'I need to be seen to be coping and in control'. Various stressful events such as her partner's death, bringing up her family alone, having a very busy job and having some physical problems could have precipitated her into the fatigued state. Maintenance factors could be pushing on, taking little rest and trying to sort out everyone's problems. I did not feel she was entirely comfortable with this formulation, but we agreed to have a trial of CBT, as she accepted there was a degree of truth in it.

In retrospect, I think there is validity in the formulation but there are things missing from it. These are in particular traumatic events that were too embarrassing to talk about; also I did not understand the extreme emotional avoidance that was at play.

My first visit for CBT consisted of a two-hour assessment. I was totally exhausted by this but very keen to get the treatment underway, and also prove that I was not mentally ill and my illness was not all in my mind. At the end of the session I was handed a piece of paper with the Therapist's evaluation of how my illness could be explained in psychological terms. A telephone consultation was arranged in a few weeks' time and I was told to balance out rest, activity and relaxation.

When I got home and read through the Therapist's notes I realised that they consisted of a summary of the main areas of stress in my life. I wondered if my illness could have been caused by stress. If so, I thought it should disappear now that I was not pushing myself any more. I felt heartened until it dawned on me that if my illness was caused by stress I must have brought it on myself. I had made myself ill. This thought angered me.

The day of the telephone consultation arrived and when I heard the Therapist's voice I broke down in tears and told him that I hated the idea that I'd made myself ill. I was told that this was not what was said and given an appointment to go to hospital for a face-to-face therapy session. At my first proper CBT session it was suggested to me that I had been in a 'boom and bust' pattern, pushing myself mercilessly to the point of collapse when I should have been interspersing activity with proper periods of total rest. Initially I was sceptical about the benefits of having a 'psychological' treatment for what I thought was a 'physical' illness, but I could not have been more wrong. I soon overcame my misgivings and over the months my CBT sessions helped me to manage my illness so as to minimise its effects. CBT turned out to be a simple and constructive therapy that works, the only down side being it was not the cure I had hoped it might be.

Early on in my treatment programme I lost my job. I was glad that my CBT Therapist was there to help me work through the conflicting emotions that job loss brings. It was useful to have impartial help and advice even though the actual decisions were always my own.

I had asked Catherine at an early stage of treatment to complete an activity diary, and it was fairly clear that she was still fairly active and busy, with occasional 'crashing out' when the symptoms were overwhelming. We focussed first of all in trying to get a balance in her life and she agreed that she would 'have a balance between activity/rest over the day and over the week'. We had agreed that this target was better than trying to get her to plan out every activity and rest in detail. The goal was to balance her activity levels to stabilise her symptoms, and to avoid severe symptoms. She would fit into the category of patients who are relatively active. I referred her to the physiotherapist and she had some sessions there of 'exercise, reflex-therapy and cranio-sacral therapy', which was helpful at the time but did not have lasting benefits. I had referred her because of her severe physical symptoms. After a few sessions of seeing me her mood dipped, and this was because she was moving to seeing the CFS as driven by psychological factors, as opposed to physical factors. This led to the thought 'I've made myself ill', and required some discussion about the interaction of the five systems of environment, cognition, mood, behaviour and physiology, and she partially accepted this.

As she got to know me, she told me about the importance of loss and how she found loss particularly painful, and this was because of the loss of her mother, Paul and other important people in her life. This was helping me develop the formulation further. I also began to understand that when she lost her job this was a great blow, not just for financial reasons but because she had invested her self-esteem in this. Some of this information came out of the use of the negative thought diaries and some from discussions. In terms of symptoms there was little improvement. I was unclear whether she was achieving a balance between rest and activity, and this happens fairly often with patients. We agreed that she was deconditioned, because having been very fit and sporty before she had been focussing on trying to do her job, and there was little time for exercise. We have indeed worked on this, and she has been doing gentle walking, exercise biking and Pilates. When we have tried to increase the pace of exercise it has led to an intolerable increase in symptoms and indeed an increase in alarming fainting episodes where she has been injured. This issue of increasing activity is complex as the research suggests that graded activity/exercise is helpful, but sometimes the formulation suggests it is not crucially important to do this, or the increase of activity leads to adverse consequences, rather than the moderate increase in symptoms one would expect. I would say that the gentle exercise programme that she has followed has not had any adverse consequences, but has not obviously improved her symptoms or functioning.

> As I continued to attend for CBT we tried various strategies, the most helpful being resting for about 75 per cent of every waking day, and for a previously busy person this was not much of a life. We were aware that I was losing my previous level of fitness so I tried to exercise as much as my illness would allow; but each and every time I over-stepped the 75 per cent rest mark the illness returned to its previous sickening level and I began to wonder if I would ever be well again.

We moved on to work with some of the underlying unhelpful rules, and developed alternatives such as 'I will respect other people's needs, but not put them before myself' and 'I am valuable even if I'm not achieving'. There has been a degree of progress with these, particularly in trying to curb excessive self-sacrificing and appeasing behaviour that was plainly contributing to the fatigue.

Catherine continued to suffer quite severe symptoms, though she had good days and bad, which did not have any apparent pattern. She frequently had viruses that worsened the fatigue, and the fainting continued along with bouts of skin complaints and other odd symptoms that were investigated by her GP without any clear cause being found. All through this she was working very conscientiously at her CBT programme.

As she got to know me and she felt more trusting she talked more about the events of Paul's illness and death and their traumatic aftermath. Paul had been torn between Catherine and his wife, and spent time with each of them. He had been diagnosed with heart disease and this led to more heartbreak. When he was terminally ill in hospital his wife came and took him home, so when Catherine came to visit him in hospital he was gone. She went to his house, but soon after that he died and she had not been able to say goodbye. On the day of the funeral, although she attended, Paul's wife excluded her from the ceremony. She was abused and shouted at by mourners from his wife's family. When she went home an individual who had been at the funeral seriously assaulted her. He was in a position of authority over her and threatened her to say nothing. This whole experience, as one can imagine, was horrible and traumatic. The only way to cope with it was to not talk or think about it because it was so difficult and she needed to cope for her children. She took the stance of pushing on, working hard, trying to make amends for being such a bad person. She also lived under constant fear of the person who assaulted her. This pattern continued for some time. There was a high degree of shame, emotional avoidance, control and suppression.

After we had spoken about this the question arose as to whether it was a good idea, or even possible, to try to deal with this material. The concern was that it would be so stressful that it would cause a significant worsening in symptoms. I referred her for a psychodynamic therapy opinion. Whilst we were waiting for this we tried to push on with the work on rules and beliefs. We made some headway with this but there seemed to be little emotional integration of the new beliefs and they were quite weakly held. It was very difficult to shift a sense of herself as being a 'bad' or 'lesser' person. On discussion with medical colleagues we tried her on an SSRI anti-depressant, then a tricyclic anti-depressant. She found both of these intolerable because of immediate adverse effects, which were quite severe. As described in Chapter 9 there is not strong evidence that anti-depressants are helpful in pure CFS, and this attempt at using medication was a pragmatic attempt to address poor progress. There was some attempt to use alternative medical approaches, but an effort to use a 'detoxification diet' led to a significant worsening of symptoms that persisted for weeks.

When the psychodynamic opinion came back, they said that it would not be advisable to do deeper work as it would be destabilising and she was unwilling to change. I was not sure about whether this opinion was correct but I accepted it, and I started to discuss working towards discharge. This was very difficult indeed for her because as she put it 'If I'm discharged I won't have any chance of getting better'. She had experienced difficult loss before. Later on she said that she felt that she really needed to address the trauma and grief and was scared of being discharged without doing this. Although the plan had been to reduce the sessions and move towards discharge, this became difficult because of developing family crises, which did not allow for any improvement in symptoms. We moved on in therapy to try to manage these crises better. Whilst we were doing this she revealed more about the traumatic events, and it was clear from what she said that she would meet the diagnosis of post-traumatic stress disorder as well as CFS. I decided to get a second CBT opinion from a respected colleague, and his very clear opinion was that it was necessary and advisable to try to deal with the traumas and grief, though it would be difficult. So at the time of writing we are going to embark on doing this.

With the CBT I have gained a better understanding of how difficult early experiences, my own attitudes and beliefs, and stressful events have contributed to my symptoms. I have made reasonable progress in dealing with these, but it is hard. Then, as time went by, I was told that my CBT sessions must come to an end whether I was better or not. As there was no other treatment on offer I felt abandoned by the medical profession at my time of greatest need. I felt anxious about the future. 'What if I never get better?' I discussed this with my Therapist who told me that, although it was actually unlikely that I would get very much better, I must remain 'realistically optimistic'.

Five years on from the onset, I still feel ill every day, I present to the world an image of coping and being reasonably cheerful and strong, but privately I feel vulnerable, weak and scared. Avoiding relapses has become an important aspect of my illness management. Viral infections and stress are particularly damaging and very hard to avoid because I seem to pick up every infection that is going around and I also find that the illness in itself is a constant source of stress. People who were sympathetic when I first became ill now treat me with disbelief; no one asks me how I am and the subject of illness is carefully avoided. Although it is usually unspoken I feel that people expect me to 'pull myself together' now and get better. Nowadays the most frequent thing people say to me is 'You look well'. This is said in an almost threatening way, as if this was the key to feeling well. I find this hurtful. To look well but feel ill is a cruel irony.

I am often asked if I am eating, exercising and sleeping properly; if I've heard of the latest herbal remedy; if I have tried healing, homeopathy, acupuncture, reiki, vitamins, evening primrose oil, co-enzyme Q10, Indian head massage, antibiotics, anti-viral, anti-candida medication... and so on, and so on. I feel like shouting at these well meaning people that if any of these things was a proven cure for CFS every doctor in the land would be prescribing them as a treatment!

On the plus side I am better able to control my illness; I learnt this skill during my CBT sessions. I now take pleasure from a completely different range of activities, but different does not necessarily mean less enjoyable. One thing is very clear, if I want to maintain any degree of recovery I must not go back to my old 'boom and bust' behaviour. My best course of action is to increase my activities very, very gradually but never to the point where they cause a serious relapse. Although this sounds quite simple it is extremely difficult in practice as there is such a fine line between doing just enough and overdoing things.

Part of me still hopes that there will be a medical breakthrough for CFS sufferers, but at the same time my realistic side accepts that CFS is an umbrella term for a number of different illnesses so a single treatment and cure are unlikely to be found.

In terms of the future of my CBT, my discharge has been postponed, and I am now working on coming to terms with some of the difficult experiences that I have had in the past, and I am hoping that this will lead to some further improvement.

Issues arising from the therapist's perspective

Formulation

An important aspect of formulation is that it should be done 'early and often'. The formulation that was done at an early stage was reasonable, but inadequate. The main reason was that Catherine did not reveal information that would have allowed it to be more accurate. It also led to me underestimating the challenges of treatment. The important point is that sometimes for reasons of embarrassment or shame patients will be unable to say certain things. It also brings up the issue of whether to follow the evidence base or the formulation. The former would stress graded exercise as an important element, but the formulation does not support this. It is probably correct as stated earlier that graded exercise is always tried but with close monitoring of its effect. It is fairly obvious with this patient that her problems were not being maintained primarily through deconditioning, though it may have been a minor factor.

Treatment versus adjustment

In reality with Catherine there has been a fairly modest improvement and, as stated earlier, effect sizes from CBT can be small. It is difficult to know how much to emphasise improvement and getting better if one is sceptical that this will happen. In this case I was more optimistic at the beginning, but I did not understand the complexities of the problem, and now I am uncertain about outcome. This made it difficult for Catherine and myself to consider discharge, as she felt she was not getting as well as had been hoped. I have heard some clinicians say that one should be quite upbeat in all cases to engage and encourage patients, and other clinicians have advised realism. I would advocate the latter, and would aim to have 'a hopeful realism'.

Working with rules and beliefs

Catherine had unhelpful rules and beliefs, and it has not been easy to modify these. It may be the case that patients who have unhelpful and ingrained beliefs are more difficult to help than patients whose fatigue can be understood in terms of more straightforward maintenance factors like poor sleep.

Therapeutic relationship

This is important with all patients but probably becomes more so with those, like Catherine, who have complex problems.

Length of treatment

Change in CFS can be slow. I have been seeing Catherine for a number of years, and this seems necessary for some patients who are complex, though it is possible to see them less frequently than the standard two-week interval.

Chapter 9

Using cognitive behavioural therapy alongside other approaches to chronic fatigue syndrome

This chapter contains:

- Integrating CBT with other approaches
- Development of services
- Potential patient pathways through services
- Research agenda for CFS

Introduction

Because of the complexity of CFS and the wide range of symptoms that occur, it seems appropriate that CBT is integrated with other approaches. These may include GP care, physician care, psychiatrist care, physiotherapy and occupational therapy approaches, drug treatments, alternative medicine, and nutrition.

Given that the cognitive behavioural therapist may be involved in or even leading the development of services, it is also useful to consider what would be an ideal service to deliver care. These topics will be discussed in this chapter.

Integration with other approaches

General practitioner care

The GP will be the first person that the patient sees with their problems. It will be the GP's role to investigate the cause of the fatigue, to make a diagnosis of CFS if the patient fits the diagnostic criteria, and to provide initial treatment and advice. This can vary between GPs, and, at the time of writing in the UK, provisional best practice guidelines from the National Institute for Clinical Excellence (NICE) have just been published. Given the chronic nature of the condition, the GP has an important role in supporting the patient, managing symptoms and directing them to services, where they exist. From the CBT perspective it can be useful to speak to the GP at the assessment stage to try to gain further information about the person. If the person then has a course of CBT, then it is important to provide a detailed letter describing factors that have been worked on, and the outcome.

The NICE guidelines recommend that the mildly affected patient is referred to specialist care in six months, moderately affected patients within three months and severely affected patients immediately.

Physician care

Some patients are referred on to physician care at the general hospital, often to the areas of general medicine, rheumatology, immunology and pain medicine. Often these are patients who have not got better from the care given by the GP. Physical medicine specialists will probably investigate the patient again to ensure they do not have another medical illness, give advice, often about graded exercise and CBT, possibly prescribe medication, and may refer the patient on either to CBT or physiotherapy if they are available. In pain medicine acupuncture, massage, physiotherapy and other approaches may be available.

Psychiatrist care

Patients may be sent down this route if they have a previous psychiatric history, or if mood symptoms predominate. The patient will be supported and treated by the psychiatrist and their team, and may be given medication.

Physiotherapy

Some patients are sent here particularly if pain and immobility are prominent. Physiotherapists work by examining individuals with impairments, functional limitations and disabilities. After establishing a diagnosis they will work to alleviate this impairment by a variety of means including instructions, exercise, manipulation, use of aids, equipment, and so on (Pagliarulo 2001). The specific types of intervention that would be used include breathing techniques, muscle stretching, massage, and building up to a gradual exercise programme (Levine, Schwartz and Furst 2003). Plainly CFS could be approached this way. There is not a strong body of research investigating CFS and physiotherapy: White and Naish (2001) obtained a good result using graded exercise provided by physiotherapists. The CBT practitioner should be able to work alongside the physiotherapist, though there may be some overlap over the issue of activity alteration, and plainly an agreed written care plan is important.

Occupational therapy

This is defined by the World Federation of Occupational Therapists as 'The treatment of physical and psychiatric conditions through specific selected activities in order to help people to reach their maximum level of function in all aspects of daily life'. Although practitioners may follow different models of occupational therapy, they will have core managerial, interactive and therapeutic skills

(Hagedorn 1995). With CFS this may include setting priorities consistent with their level of function, working with body positioning, organising home and work adaptations, working with cognitive problems, and planning activity and exercise programmes (Levine, Schwartz and Furst 2003). Diane Cox has written a book developing a CBT approach to occupational therapy with CFS (Cox 2000). Again, patients may be referred to specific occupational therapy services often to help them to adapt to their problems. There is overlap with CBT, and the importance of a clear care plan and the clarification of individual responsibilities is stressed.

Drug treatments

Whiting et al (2001) reviewed the use of medications. Regarding hydrocortisone and immunoglobulin, the conclusion is that 'they have shown some limited effects but... overall evidence is inconclusive'. There is insufficient evidence around the other drugs that have been tried, including anti-depressants, to draw any conclusion. Reviewing the literature that has appeared since Whiting et al's review does not provide evidence of a breakthrough treatment, but several lines of enquiry are being followed, for example the use of stimulants. Unfortunately therefore there is not a drug that can cure the condition. Aside from trying to treat the condition patients will also be given drugs like painkillers to relieve the severity of the symptoms. The NICE guidelines state that there is no drug that is curative of CFS, and symptoms should be managed by conventional practice. They give more detailed advice in their guidelines (NICE 2006).

Alternative medicine

Because conventional medicine is not tremendously successful in helping these patients, they often seek help from the alternative sector, and the treatments pursued include acupuncture, homeopathy, and using supplements such as vitamins and minerals. Whiting et al (2001) report that homeopathy, massage and osteopathy have been studied in poorly controlled trials. Their conclusion was that there was insufficient evidence about their effectiveness.

However, many of these other approaches have not been researched, and their potential effectiveness is unknown. If a patient discusses alternative approaches one could help them look at the pros and cons of pursuing the one they were interested in. This would include looking at any experience that the patient (or the clinician) had of it being helpful, any research that has been done in the area, the credibility of the approach, and the cost.

Nutritional approaches

Whiting et al (2001) reported studies that had shown beneficial effects from the use of fatty acids and magnesium, but concluded there was 'insufficient evidence for effectiveness'. Van Konynenburg (2003) looked at the issue again arguing for the importance of nutrition. This author would agree that it is prudent, as he suggests, to ensure that one's patients are eating a balanced diet, and choosing a variety of foods from within the food groups of carbohydrate, fat and protein. Current general advice is that there should be an emphasis on eating low fat foods such as fruit, vegetables, high fibre breads and cereals, and small or modest amounts of lean meat, chicken or fish. It is also helpful to ensure that patients are not overweight as this could contribute to their symptoms. Van Konynenburg (2003) suggests that a high protein, low carbohydrate, low fat diet be tried and supplemented by a variety of vitamins and minerals as listed in his chapter. Again one would try to help the patient look at the pros and cons of nutritional approaches.

It is recommended by NICE that patients should be supported in following a well balanced diet, that patients should be referred to a dietician if they have severe weight loss, and gastrointestinal symptoms should be managed conventionally (NICE 2006).

Development of services

In the UK the National Health Service is investing in the development of CFS services. An important first stage in this was the publication of the Department of Health's 'Independent Working Group's Report into Chronic Fatigue Syndrome/ Myalgic Encephalomyelitis (CFS/ME)', published in 2002. The key conclusions were that:

- Professionals should recognise it as a chronic illness, and be willing to help those affected
- Early recognition and an authoritative diagnosis will improve outcomes
- All patients need appropriate clinical evaluation and follow-up, preferably by a multidisciplinary team
- Most care can be provided by GPs, and the quality of support, empathy and understanding provided is important
- The severely affected will require home services
- There is a lack of good quality research
- Potential useful strategies are exercise/activity programmes, cognitive behavioural therapy and pacing
- Patients can play an active role in their care and the voluntary sector can provide support

There was further information provided about young sufferers. The report was welcomed on publication, and led to government proposals for co-ordinating centres and local teams. A sum of 8.5 million pounds was invested, and a call was put out to bid for this money, to develop creative proposals and demonstrate new ways of working. Emphasis was put, in the proposal document, on creating a new service working in partnership with patients and providers, with the correct mix of staff to provide patient centred care (Source: Department of Health website).

Clinical Network Co-ordinating Centres (CNCCs) have now been set up in the UK, and they have the following aims: supporting the development of more localised multidisciplinary teams (MDTs); providing access to specialist management; providing specialist advice for complex patients; training teams; ensuring transitions between children and adult services; partnerships with voluntary organisations; disseminating best practice; and liaison with purchasers of services. They will also be expected to contribute towards: educational programmes for professionals; care packages for those with severe presentations; and developing research capacity.

The local MDTs have the following aims: to lead services in primary care; to provide patient care; to provide help for coping, adjusting and rehabilitation; to develop domiciliary services for those who are house/bed bound; to develop information and self-management techniques; to collaborate with the CNCC; and to build on existing services (Source: Department of Health website). In simple terms the CNCCs have an overseeing role and the local MDTs are providing and developing services locally.

In 2004 NICE began a process of assessing what works best in the areas of: assessment and diagnosis; adjustment and coping; symptom management; use of rehabilitation strategies geared towards optimising functioning; and achieving greater independence (Source: Department of Health website). Their provisional guideline has now been published online (NICE 2006).

It is plain that there are a variety of developments that potentially could improve the care of CFS sufferers. In terms of setting up and developing an ideal local service the following points based on clinicians' and patients' experiences may be important.

Patients' pathway

The patients' pathway describes the route that patients take through the health system. As has been noted the management of CFS often falls through the gap between physical and psychological services, and there is often a lack of clarity over who should take responsibility. General practitioners will see the patient first, and this service can be variable. In the past, patients were sometimes told that there was 'no such thing as chronic fatigue' or 'it's all in your mind'. Patients may be managed in the surgery, or sent to physiotherapists, physicians or psychologists depending on the GP's views. One study (Raine, Carter, Sensky and Black 2004) found that GPs stereotyped CFS patients as having undesirable traits: this was because of the lack of a clear bodily location of the problem, the way the syndrome has been reclassified over the years, and the patients' inability to fit into a standard 'sick role'. This leads to management difficulties. Most GPs and clinicians try to do a good job with a condition that is hard to understand and treat, and where there has been a lack of clear guidelines. Some patients are sent on to secondary care in the general hospital, and again the service has been variable.

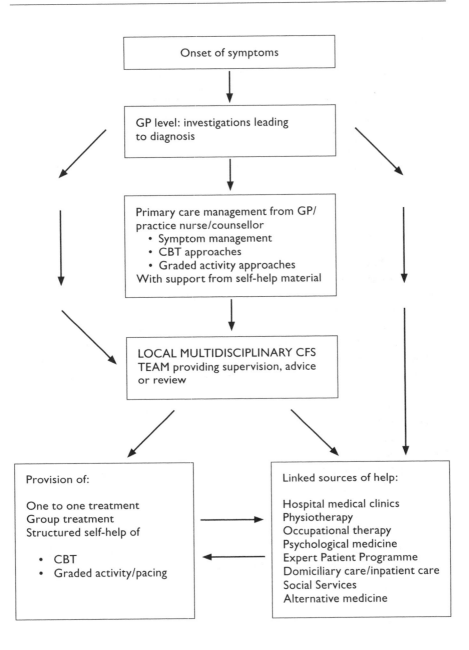

Figure 9.1 A possible patient pathway.

A good patient pathway (Figure 9.1) will ensure that the patient travels through the pathway and receives the correct care.

The pathway is that patients are seen at GP level, investigated and either managed at primary care level or referred to the CFS MDT, or referred to more specialised services like physical medicine, psychological medicine or the 'Expert Patient Programme'. The role of the MDT would be to provide advice/supervision or actual review of the patient, possibly dependent on their resources. They would then utilise a programme of care either using CBT/graded activity/pacing after an assessment or alternative approaches external or internal to the team. All services would review progress and discharge back to the GP. Potential problems may be the GP's uncertainty about diagnosis, uncertainty or lack of skill in managing patients at primary care level, reluctance of other services such as physical or psychological medicine to be involved, and inadequate resources within the CFS MDT to meet demand.

Staff skill mix

Recommendations from the Department of Health are that the MDT should manage CFS. In other words, that there should be a variety of staff from different disciplines who are devising and implementing an agreed care plan. The evidence base would support CBT and graded exercise. One would expect a role for a cognitive behavioural therapist who should be able to implement both of these (this person could be from any profession but should be accredited in CBT, in the UK by the British Association of Behavioural and Cognitive Psychotherapy). Similarly a physiotherapist, occupational therapist, nurse or other professional could also implement graded activity. As stated earlier the physiotherapist may utilise hands-on techniques like manipulation and acupuncture. The occupational therapist as described earlier would have a role in rehabilitation and adaptation to symptoms. It would be useful if one member of the team had expertise in exercise physiology and therapy, of which there are training modules available. The medical role in the team may be that of consultation, diagnosis, exclusion of other physical illness, political leadership, and being a 'champion' for the service. It would be wise to ensure that the team meets regularly and offers support to one another, as one would anticipate possible burnout in a group where there may not be immediate satisfactions. It is also important that proper supervision arrangements are in place for all staff, particularly to give them the chance to discuss complex patients. It would be helpful for staff to have access to gym equipment and a swimming pool, for their patients to use.

Patient involvement

Advice from the Department of Health quite correctly supports the role of patient involvement. There are various support groups who are keen to provide input, and do so to a high standard. The patient groups rightly or wrongly tend to have a more 'physical' view of the condition, are less keen on psychological input, and are drawn to alternative approaches; some may wish to see research focussed on biological causes and treatments. This can cause some tension with service providers.

Research agenda

The Medical Research Council has developed a broad strategy for advancing health service and biomedical research in CFS/ME (Medical Research Council CFS/ME Research Advisory Group 2003). They suggested that there were a number of areas for research:

- Case definition, the problem being the lack of a universally agreed diagnostic criterion
- Population studies, looking at incidence, causation, triggers and outcomes
- Disease development; potential areas are infections, neurology, muscle fatigue, weakness, immunology, neuro-endocrinology, central nervous system, intellectual performance and psychological factors
- Useful treatment. They identified that graded exercise and CBT show promise, and further work needs to be done on rehabilitative and psychological treatments

They emphasise that research should be multidisciplinary and should involve patient representatives. They are currently supporting a large study comparing CBT, graded activity and pacing.

Looking to the future

The author's experience is that there have been some improvements in the care of CFS patients in the UK, particularly in the sense that it is more accepted as a condition, and there are more plans for its management. However treatment effects from CBT and graded exercise are rather small. Many patients are left with considerable disability. One would hope that in the future behavioural treatments would become more refined. It is also hoped that biological research would lead to drug treatments that may have a beneficial impact.

In the future one would like to see increased provision of service, rehabilitation strategies targeted specifically at the CFS group, practical help for people who do not recover or have severe presentations, and more of a dialogue between the people who are researching the condition purely from a biological or psychological perspective. In the end these developments would assist the sufferers who have this disabling condition.

Chapter summary

As recommended, CBT would have a role within an MDT approach to CFS. This MDT could involve the general practitioner, the physician, the psychiatrist, the physiotherapist and the occupational therapist. Services have been developed in the UK, with the setting up of CNCCs and also local MDTs for adults and children. Patient pathways through these services are being planned. It has been advocated that more research is needed focussing on case definition, population studies, disease development and useful treatments.

Appendix 3.1

ASSESSMENT PROMPT SHEET

Consider the information provided in the original referral and use that to consider a potential formulation and how the therapeutic relationship can be initially developed.

Explain the goal of the interview, the duration and ask if the person shares that goal and if there is anything that they wish to say before the assessment.

Ask for a general description of the main problems.

Ask for specific details about the main problems (one would expect the patient to talk about specific symptoms). Use the idea of frequency, intensity and trigger.

Ask about potential *maintenance* factors.

Ask about psychological maintenance factors:

(a) Stressful general events and cognitive, emotional and behavioural responses to them.

(b) The experience of CFS and cognitive, emotional and behavioural responses to this.

Ask about sleep problems.

Enquire if they have physical illnesses.

Enquire if they have problems with viruses.

Consider asking whether previous advice has been unhelpful in any way. Consider asking whether the patient has any reasons not to get better, and consider the best way of asking about this.

Evaluate *precipitating* factors: trace the onset and history of the problem. Why is the person coming for help at this time?

Ask about medication, alcohol, drug and caffeine use.

Consider *predisposing and precipitating* factors. Complete the personal history covering: medical, psychiatric and forensic history; personality; living arrangements, financial situation and hobbies; parents and siblings; upbringing, education and work history; relationships, marriage and sexual history; religion.

Conduct a mental state examination and assess risk.

Consider diagnosis, formulation and suitability for the CBT approach. Consider whether any further information needs to be sought before conclusions can be drawn.

Appendix 3.2

BALANCE SHEET

Most restful occupations			Most tiring occupations

Instructions to patients: list all your occupations and place on the grid.

Appendix 3.3

ACTIVITY DIARY: FREQUENCY, INTENSITY AND TRIGGERS OF YOUR PHYSICAL SYMPTOMS

Please fill this diary in by writing what you are doing each hour (so we can look for triggers); what symptoms you have if any and how intense they are on a scale of 0 being no symptoms and 10 being the most intense they could be.

Time	Mon	Tue	Wed	Thurs	Fri	Sat	Sun
7–8am							
8–9am							
9–10am							
10–11am							
11–12 noon							
12–1pm							
1–2pm							

Time	Mon	Tue	Wed	Thurs	Fri	Sat	Sun
2–3pm							
3–4pm							
4–5pm							
5–6pm							
6–7pm							
7–8pm							
8–9pm							
9–10pm							
10–11pm							
11–12 midnight							
Any Other Time							

Appendix 3.4

SLEEP DIARY

Please complete this diary every morning for one week:

	Mon	Tue	Wed	Thu	Fri	Sat	Sun
I went to bed at ... o'clock and turned the lights out at ... o'clock							
After turning the lights out I fell asleep in ... minutes							
My sleep was interrupted ... times through the night							
My sleep was interrupted for ... minutes in total							

	Mon	Tue	Wed	Thu	Fri	Sat	Sun
I finally woke at …							
I got out of bed at …							
Overall my sleep last night was … (0=sound, 8=very restless)							
When I got up this morning I felt … (0=refreshed, 8=exhausted)							
Other comments							

Appendix 3.5

PROBLEM AND GOAL RATING SHEET

NAME

Pre/Post/ 1mfu/3mfu/6mfu/1yr

PROBLEM A

PROBLEM B

PROBLEM C

RATING KEY

This problem upsets me/interferes with my normal activities

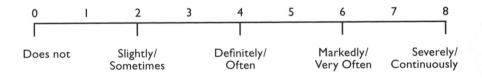

0	1	2	3	4	5	6	7	8
Does not		Slightly/ Sometimes		Definitely/ Often		Markedly/ Very Often		Severely/ Continuously

GOAL A1   ☐

GOAL A2   ☐

GOAL A3   ☐

GOAL B1   ☐

GOAL B2   ☐

GOAL B3   ☐

GOAL B4   ☐

GOAL C1   ☐

GOAL C2   ☐

GOAL C3   ☐

GOAL C4   ☐

RATING KEY

My progress towards achieving this goal regularly without difficulty

0	1	2	3	4	5	6	7	8

Complete   75% success   50% success   25% success   No success
success

Appendix 3.6

BEHAVIOURAL CHANGE SHEET

The purpose of a behavioural change will be to help you learn something or think about something in a different way; or to help you reach your longer term goals; or improve some element of your functioning like sleep or fitness. When we agree a behavioural change it is better to write it in the first person, to be specific, and to set a frequency or time limit.

When you are writing what the behavioural changes are remember to think about: What is the purpose of this change? What will be the difficulties in doing it? How can I overcome these difficulties?

(1)

(2)

(3)

(4)

(5)

(6)

(7)

(8)

(9)

(10)

Appendix 5.1

NEGATIVE THOUGHT DIARY

Situation	Mood	Negative Automatic Thoughts
Write a brief description of the situation that triggered your thoughts and feelings	Use one word to describe the mood you had (e.g. anxiety, depression, guilt, shame, anger, etc.). Rate it on a scale of 100%	Write down what was going through your mind just before you had this mood. Try to find the upsetting thought that led to the mood

Evidence that Supports the Negative Thought	Evidence that Challenges the Negative Thought	Balanced Thought
Write down evidence that supports the negative thought	Write down the answers to each of the following questions: (1) What evidence does not support the negative thought? (2) Is there another way of looking at this? (3) Why is it not helpful to think like this? What 'thinking error' am I making (if any)? (4) What would I say to my best friend who had this thought?	Write down a short statement that counterbalances the original negative thought MOOD Now re-rate your mood on a scale of 0–100%

HELP IN COMPLETING THE NEGATIVE THOUGHT DIARY

1   Become aware of a change in your mood, and if this is an unhealthy mood, please complete the diary.
2   Write the mood down, alongside the situation that triggered it off.
3   Write down what was going through your mind just before you had this mood. It would be helpful if you could try to find the upsetting thought that led to this mood. The main way to do this is to repeatedly ask this question until you have a sense that you have got to the 'bottom line'. For example; the person feels depressed at 70 per cent because his brother did not phone as expected. He follows the diary procedure and asks himself, 'What was going through my mind just before I felt depressed?' His initial thought was 'It's that my brother hasn't phoned'. He then asks 'What is there about my brother not phoning tonight that's making me depressed?' He immediately thinks, 'It's because he doesn't want anything to do with me because I'm ill', and he realises that he has uncovered the key negative thought that is making him depressed.
4   Once you understand this part of the diary move on to the next section.
5   State what factual evidence you have that backs up the negative thought.
6   Use the questions to find as much evidence you can against the negative thought. Try to decide whether you are engaged in one of the following thinking errors.

   a. Emotional reasoning – believing something about yourself, others or the future purely based on an emotion. It is important to remember that being in a depressed mood makes us focus on loss and failure, and being in an anxious mood makes us focus on threat.
   b Over-generalising – jumping from one specific incidence to a general conclusion.
   c. Black and white thinking – being unable to see shades of grey.
   d Fortune telling – making guesses about what will happen in the future without proper consideration.
   e. Mind-reading – again, making guesses about what someone else believes without proper consideration.
   f. Catastrophising – overestimating the riskiness and badness of a situation, because you are in an anxious state.

7   Try now to find a balanced thought that is realistic and helpful. Then re-rate your mood.
8   Consider yourself and discuss with your therapist whether you need to do something about your balanced thought.
9   Remember that it takes a while to master doing the diary. It is not a test of you or your spelling or punctuation.

Appendix 5.2

BELIEF AND RULE WORKBOOK

OLD BELIEF

What is the old belief or rule?

Where did the belief or rule come from and how has it been reinforced over the years? (Consider your upbringing and patterns of behaviour)

What effect has the belief or rule had on your life? (Think of the disadvantages and any advantages)

How do I know that the belief or rule is active? (Think about your mood, thoughts, behaviours and relationships)

What is the evidence that the belief or rule is not completely true? (Write down as much evidence as you can that the belief is not completely true, firstly in your present life and then looking back through all stages of your life)

1)

2)

3)

4)

5)

6)

7)

8)

9)

10)

Why is this belief or rule unhelpful to me?
(Consider the effect on your mood, behaviour, symptoms, work and
relationships)

1)

2)

3)

4)

5)

6)

7)

8)

9)

10)

11)

Collect evidence on a daily basis that runs counter to the old belief or rule.

DATE	EVIDENCE

NEW BELIEF

What is the new belief or rule?

What is the evidence that the new belief or rule is truer and more helpful? (Try to provide additional evidence that you have not considered before)

1)

2)

3)

4)

5)

6)

Devise behavioural changes that support the new belief or rule.

1)

2)

3)

4)

5)

Glossary of CBT/CFS terminology

Aerobic exercise Exercise, such as brisk walking, that leads to increased oxygen consumption, primarily benefiting the cardiovascular system.

Anaerobic exercise Exercise that draws upon the muscles' own stores of energy and does not require oxygen, such as weight-lifting.

(Core) belief In CBT, a fixed attitude about the self, others and the world that may be unhelpful to the individual, for example 'I am lazy'.

Deconditioning A decline in physical fitness, as from a period of inactivity.

Formulation A way of relating CBT theory to patient presentation of symptoms. A means of making sense of the patient's problems in terms of thoughts, moods, physical reactions, behaviours and environment.

Homework In CBT, tasks that are given to the patient to do between sessions, and which may include collecting information, challenging unhelpful thoughts and beliefs, and changing unhelpful behaviours.

Iatrogenic A condition that has arisen from medical intervention.

Negative automatic thought An individual's misappraisal of a particular situation associated with a negative mood state.

Pacing (also called activity scheduling) Having a balance of daily activities in a way that severe symptoms do not occur, and there is a gradual increase in the person's energy and stamina.

Personality disorders A group of psychological disorders in which the individual's way of perceiving, relating to or thinking about one's environment interferes with their long term functioning.

Rule (for living) In CBT, a way in which the person thinks they should act or believes things should happen that applies across a wide range of situations, for example 'I should always do things perfectly'.

Socratic questioning In CBT, a type of dialogue that one has with the patient to help draw out their own opinions and considerations.

Thinking errors The way in which an individual mentally processes information when they are in a particular emotional state, for example catastrophising when anxious.

References

Abbey, S. E. (1996). Psychotherapeutic perspectives on chronic fatigue syndrome. In Demitrack, M. A. and Abbey, S. E. (eds) *Chronic Fatigue Syndrome*. New York: Guilford, pp. 185–211.

Afari, N. and Buchwald, D. (2003). Chronic fatigue syndrome: a review. *American Journal of Psychiatry*, 160(2), 221–236.

American Psychiatric Association (1995). *Diagnostic and Statistical Manual of Mental Disorders*. Washington, DC: American Psychiatric Association.

Anthony, M. M. and Swinson, R. P. (1998). *When Perfect Isn't Good Enough*. Oakland, CA: New Harbinger.

Antoni, M. H. and Weiss, D. E. (2003). Stress and immunity. In Jason, L. A., Fennell, P. A. and Taylor, R. R. (eds) *Handbook of Chronic Fatigue Syndrome*. New York: Wiley, pp. 527–545.

Bazelmans, E., Bleijenberg, G., van der Meer, J. W. and Folgering, H. (2001). Is physical deconditioning a perpetuating factor in chronic fatigue syndrome? A controlled study on maximal exercise performance and relations with fatigue, impairment, and physical activity. *Psychological Medicine*, 31, 107–114.

Beck, A. T. (1976). *Cognitive Therapy and the Emotional Disorders*. New York: Madison.

Beck, A. T., Ward C. H., Mendelson, M., Mock, J. and Erbaugh, J. (1961). An inventory for measuring depression. *Archives of General Psychiatry*, 4, 561–571.

Beck, A. T., Rush, A. J., Shaw, B. F. and Emery, G. (1979). *Cognitive Therapy of Depression*. New York: Guilford.

Benca, R. M., Obermeyer, W. H., Shelton, S. E., Droster, J. and Kalin, N. H. (2000). Effects of amygdala lesions on sleep in rhesus monkeys. *Brain Research*, 879(1–2), 130–138.

Blackburn, I. and Twaddle, V. (1996). *Cognitive Therapy in Action*. London: Souvenir Press.

Bleijenberg, G., Prins, J. and Bazelmans, E. (2003). Cognitive behavioural approaches. In Jason, A. J., Fennell, P. A. and Taylor R. R. (eds) *Handbook of Chronic Fatigue Syndrome*. New York: Wiley, pp. 493–526.

Blenkiron, P., Edwards, R. and Lynch, S. (1999). Associations between perfectionism, mood, and fatigue in chronic fatigue syndrome: a pilot study. *Journal of Nervous and Mental Disease*, 187(9), 566–570.

Buchwald, D. (1996). Fibromyalgia and chronic fatigue syndrome: similarities and differences. *Rheumatic Disease Clinics of North America*, 22, 219–243.

Buchwald, D. and Garrity, D. (1994). Comparison of patients with chronic fatigue syndrome, fibromyalgia, and multiple chemical sensitivities. *Archives of Internal Medicine*, 154, 2049–2053.

Buchwald, D., Pascualy, R., Bombardier, C. and Kith, P. (1994). Sleep disorders in patients with chronic fatigue. *Clinical Infectious Diseases*, 18, 68–72.

Buckley, L., MacHale, S. M., Cavanagh, J. T. O., Sharpe, M., Deary, I. J. and Lawrie, S. M. (1999). Personality dimensions in chronic fatigue syndrome and depression. *Journal of Psychosomatic Research,* 46(4), 395–400.

Burgess, M. and Chalder, T. (2005). *Overcoming Chronic Fatigue*. London: Robinson.

Burnet, R. B. and Chatterton, B. E. (2001). Gastro-intestinal symptoms and gastric emptying studies in chronic fatigue syndrome [Abstract]. *Proceedings of the Third International Clinical and Scientific Meeting on Myalgic Encephalopathy/Chronic Fatigue Syndrome*. Alison Hunter Memorial Foundation, PO Box 2093, BOWRAL NSW 2576, Australia.

Burnett, C. K. and Drossman, D. A. (2004). Irritable bowel syndrome and other functional gastrointestinal disorders. In Haas, L. J. (ed.) *Handbook of Primary Care Psychology*. New York: Oxford University Press, pp. 411–424.

Candy, B., Chalder, T., Cleare, A. J., Peakman, A., Skowera, A., Wessely, S., Weinman, J., Zuckerman M. and Hotopf, M. (2003). Predictors of fatigue following the onset of infectious mononucleosis. *Psychological Medicine*, 33(5), 847–855.

Chalder, T. (1995). *Coping with Chronic Fatigue*. London: Sheldon.

Chalder, T., Berelowitz, G., Pawlikowska, T., Watts, L., et al (1993). Development of a fatigue scale. *Journal of Psychosomatic Research,* 37(2), 147–153.

Christodoulou, C., DeLuca, J., Johnson, S. K., Lange, G., Gaudino, E. A. and Natelson, B. H. (1999). Examination of Cloninger's basic dimensions of personality in fatiguing illness: Chronic fatigue syndrome and multiple sclerosis. *Journal of Psychosomatic Research*, 47(6), 597–607.

Clark, D. A. and Steer, R. A. (1996). Empirical status of the cognitive model of anxiety and depression. In Salkovskis, P. M. (ed.) *Frontiers of Cognitive Therapy*. New York: Guilford, pp. 75–96.

Cleare, A. J. (2003). The neuroendocrinology of chronic fatigue syndrome. *Endocrine Reviews*, 24(2), 236–252.

Cole, F., MacDonald, H., Carus, C. and Howden Leach, H. (2005). *Overcoming Chronic Pain*. London: Robinson.

Convertino, V. (1997). Exercise and adaptation to microgravity environments. In Fregly, J. and Blatteis, C. (eds) *Handbook of Physiology: Adaptation to the Environment*. Bethesda, MD: American Physiological Society, pp. 815–843.

Cope, H., Mann, A., Pelosi, A. and David, A. (1996). Psychosocial risk factors for chronic fatigue and chronic fatigue syndrome following presumed viral illness: A case-control study. *Psychological Medicine,* 26(6), 1197–1209.

Cox, D. (2000). *Occupational Therapy and Chronic Fatigue Syndrome*. London: Whurr.

Darnley, S. and Millar, B. (2003). *Understanding Irritable Bowel Syndrome*. Chichester: Wiley.

Deale, A., Chalder, T., Marks, I. and Wessely, S. (1997). Cognitive behavior therapy for chronic fatigue syndrome: a randomized controlled trial. *American Journal of Psychiatry*, 154, 408–414.

Deale, A., Husain, K., Chalder, T. and Wessely, S. (2001). Long term outcome of cognitive behavior therapy versus relaxation therapy for chronic fatigue syndrome; a five year follow up study. *American Journal of Psychiatry*, 158, 2038–2042.

Demitrack, M. A. and Abbey, S. E. (1996). *Chronic Fatigue Syndrome: An Integrative Approach to Evaluation and Treatment*. London: Guilford.

Department of Health (2001). *Treatment Choice in Psychological Therapies*. London: Department of Health.

Department of Health (2002). *Independent Working Group's Report into Chronic Fatigue Syndrome/Myalgic Encephalomyelitis (CFS/ME)*. London: Department of Health.

D'Zurilla, T. J. and Nezu, A. M. (2000). *Problem Solving Therapy*. New York: Springer.

Eimer, B. N. and Freeman, A. M. (1998). *Pain Management Psychotherapy: A Practical Guide*. Hoboken: Wiley.

Ellis, A. (1962). *Reason and Emotion in Psychotherapy*. Secaucus, NJ: Lyle Stuart.

Espie, C. A. (2002). Insomnia: Conceptual issues in the development, persistence, and treatment of sleep disorder in adults. *Annual Review of Psychology*, 53(1), 215–243.

Evans, B. W., Clark, W. K., Moore, D. J. and Whorell, P. J. (2005). Tegaserod for the treatment of irritable bowel syndrome (Cochrane review). *The Cochrane Library, Issue Two*. Chichester: Wiley.

Fennell, M. (1999). *Overcoming Low Self Esteem*. London: Robinson.

Fennell, P. A. (2003). A four phase approach to understanding chronic fatigue syndrome. In Jason, A. J., Fennell, P. A. and Taylor, R. R. (eds) *Handbook of Chronic Fatigue Syndrome*. New York: Wiley, pp. 455–492.

Fisher, L. (2003). Childhood experiences of illness and parenting in adults with chronic fatigue syndrome. *Journal of Psychosomatic Research*, 54, 439–443.

Ford, D. E. and Kamerow, D. B. (1989). Epidemiologic study of sleep disturbances and psychiatric disorders. *Journal of the American Medical Association*, 262, 1479–1484.

Fulcher, K. Y and White, P. D. (1997). Randomised controlled trial of graded exercise in patients with the chronic fatigue syndrome. *British Journal of Medicine*, 314, 1647–1652.

Gordon, N. F. (1993). *Chronic Fatigue: Your Complete Exercise Guide*. Leeds: Human Kinetics Publishing.

Gouldsmit, E. (2003). Review of 'The handbook of chronic fatigue syndrome'. http://www.cfids-cab.org/MESA/Goudsmit.html. Accessed 8th November 2006.

Grafman, J. (1994). Neurophysiological features of chronic fatigue syndrome. In Straus, S. E. (ed.) *Chronic Fatigue Syndrome*. New York: Marcel Dekker, pp. 263–283.

Greenberger, D. and Padesky, C. (1995). *Mind over Mood*. New York: Guilford.

Grossman, P., Niemann, L., Schmidt, S. and Wallach, H. (2004). Mindfulness-based stress reduction and health benefits: A meta-analysis. *Journal of Psychosomatic Research*, 57(1), 35–43.

Hagedorn, R. (1995). *Occupational Therapy: Perspectives and Processes*. Oxford: Churchill Livingstone.

Hatcher, S. and House, A. (2003). Life events, difficulties and dilemmas in the onset of chronic fatigue syndrome: A case-control study. *Psychological Medicine*, 33(7), 1185–1192.

Hawkins, R. M. F. (2001). A systematic meta review of hypnosis as an empirically supported treatment for pain. *Pain Reviews*, 8(2), 47–73.

Hawton, K., Salkovskis, P. M., Kirk, J. and Clark, D. M. (1989). *Cognitive Behavioural Therapy for Psychiatric Problems: A Practical Guide*. Oxford: Oxford University Press.

Heap, M. and Aravind, K. A. K. (2001). *Hartland's Medical and Dental Hypnosis*. London: Churchill Livingstone.

Henderson, M. and Tannock, C. (2004). Objective assessment of personality disorder in chronic fatigue syndrome. *Journal of Psychosomatic Research*, 56(2), 251–254.

Herbert, M. (1997). Sleep, circadian rhythms and health. In Baum, A., Newman, S., Wienman, J. and McManus C. (eds) *The Cambridge Handbook of Psychology, Health and Medicine*. Cambridge: Cambridge University Press, pp. 165–167.

Holmes, G. P., Kaplan, J. E., Gantz, N. M., Komaroff, A. L., Schonberger, L. B., Straus S. E., et al (1988). Chronic fatigue syndrome: a working case definition. *Annals of Internal Medicine*, 108, 387–389.

Huibers, M. J., Beurskens, A. J. H .M., van Schayck, C. P., Bazelmans, E., Metsemakers-Job, F. M., Knottnerus, J. A. and Bleijenberg, G. (2004). Efficacy of cognitive-behavioural therapy by general practitioners for unexplained fatigue among employees: Randomised controlled trial. *British Journal of Psychiatry*, 184(3), 240–246.

Hyde, B. (2003). The complexities of diagnosis. In Jason, A. J., Fennell, P. A. and Taylor, R. R. *Handbook of Chronic Fatigue Syndrome.* New York: Wiley, pp. 42–72.

Jacobson, N. S., Dobson, K. S., Truax, P. A., Addis, M. E., Koerner, K., Gollan, J. K., Gortner, E. and Prince, S. E. (1996). A component analysis of cognitive-behavioral treatment for depression. *Journal of Consulting and Clinical Psychology,* 64(2), 295–304.

Jason, A. J., Fennell, P. A. and Taylor, R. R. (2003). *Handbook of Chronic Fatigue Syndrome.* New York: Wiley.

Jason, L. A., Richman, J. A., Rademaker, A. W., Jordan, K .M., Plioplys, A. V., Taylor, R. R., McCready, W., Huang, C. F. and Plioplys, S (1999). A community based study of chronic fatigue syndrome. *Archives of Internal Medicine,* 18, 2129–2137.

Johnson, S. K., DeLuca, J. and Natelson, B. H. (1996). Depression in fatiguing illness: comparing patients with chronic fatigue syndrome, multiple sclerosis and depression. *Journal of Affective Disorders,* 39(1), 21–30.

Johnson, S. K., Lange, G., Tiersky, L., DeLuca, J. and Natelson, B. H. (2001). Health-related personality variables in chronic fatigue syndrome and multiple sclerosis. *Journal of Chronic Fatigue Syndrome,* 8(3–4), 41–52.

Kabatt-Zinn, J. (2004). *Full Catastrophe Living.* New York: Piatkus.

Kellner, R. (1991). *Psychosomatic Syndromes and Somatic Symptoms.* Washington, DC: American Psychiatric Association.

Kinsella, P. (2002). Review: behavioural interventions show the most promise for chronic fatigue syndrome. *Evidence Based Nursing,* 5(2), 46.

Kroese, A. (1977). The effect of inactivity on reactive hyperemia in the human calf: A study with strain gauge plethysmography. *Scandanavian Journal of Clinical Laboratory Investigation,* 37, 53–58.

Lackner, J. M., Mesmer, C., Morley, S., Dowzer, C. and Hamilton, S. (2004). Psychological treatments for irritable bowel syndrome: A systematic review and meta-analysis. *Journal of Consulting and Clinical Psychology,* 72(6), 1100–1113.

Lapp, C. W. (2000). The role of laboratory tests in diagnosis of chronic fatigue syndrome. *CFS Research Review,* 1(1), 6–88

Leahy, R. L. and Holland, S. J. (2000). *Treatment Plans and Interventions for Depression and Anxiety Disorders.* New York: Guilford.

Levine, P., Schwartz, S. and Furst, G. (2003). Medical intervention and management. In Jason, L. A., Fennell, P. A. and Taylor, R. R. (eds) *Handbook of Chronic Fatigue Syndrome.* New York. Wiley, pp. 441–454.

Lloyd, A., Hickie, A., Brockman, A., Hickie, C., Wilson, A., Dwyer, J. and Wakefield, D. (1993). Immunologic and psychologic therapy for patients with chronic fatigue syndrome: a double blind placebo controlled trial. *American Journal of Medicine,* 94, 197–203.

Magnusson, A. E., Nias, D. K. B. and White, P. D. (1996). Is perfectionism associated with fatigue? *Journal of Psychosomatic Research,* 41(4), 377–383.

Masuda, A., Nakayama, T., Yamanaka, T., Koga, Y. and Tei, C. (2002). The prognosis after multidisciplinary treatment for patients with postinfectious chronic fatigue syndrome and noninfectious chronic fatigue syndrome. *Journal of Behavioral Medicine,* 25(5), 487–497.

McCrone, P., Ridsdale, L., Darbishire, L. and Seed, P. (2004). Cost-effectiveness of cognitive behavioural therapy, graded exercise and usual care for patients with chronic fatigue in primary care. *Psychological Medicine,* 34(6), 991–999.

McCully, K. (2003). Functional capacity evaluation. In Jason, L. A., Fennell, P. A., Taylor, R. R. (eds) *Handbook of Chronic Fatigue Syndrome.* New York: Wiley, pp. 384–400.

Medical Research Council CFS/ME Research Advisory Group (2003). *CFS Research Strategy.* London: Medical Research Council.

Meier, M., Benton, A. and Diller, L. (1987). *Neuropsychological Rehabilitation.* New York: Guilford.

Melzack, R. and Wall, P. D. (1965). Pain mechanisms: A new theory. *Science*, 150, 971–979.

Melzack, R. and Wall, P. D. (1982). *The Challenge of Pain*. New York: Basic Books.

Moorey, S., Greer, S., Bliss, J. and Law, M. (1998). A comparison of adjuvant psychological therapy and supportive counselling in patients with cancer. *Psycho-oncology*, 7(3), 218–228.

Morriss, R., Sharpe, M., Sharpley, A., Cowen, P., Hawton, K. and Morris J. (1993). Abnormalities of sleep in patients with the chronic fatigue syndrome. *British Medical Journal*, 306, 1161–1164.

Mulrow, C. D., Ramirez, G., Cornell, J. E. and Allsup, K. (2001). *Defining and Managing Chronic Fatigue Syndrome. Evidence Report: Technology Assessment*. Rockville, MD: US Department of Health and Human Services.

Neenan, M. and Dryden, W. (2002). *Life Coaching: A Cognitive Behavioural Approach*. London: Routledge.

NICE: National Institute for Clinical Excellence (2006). Draft for consultation – Chronic fatigue syndrome/myalgic encephalomyelitis (or encephalopathy): Diagnosis and management of CFS/ME in adults and children. http://www.nice.org.uk/page. aspx?o=368933. Accessed 10th November 2006.

Ogden, J. (2004). *Health Psychology: A Textbook*. London: Open University Press.

Ohrbach, R. K. (1996). Stress reactivity, adaptation and response specificity in individuals with chronic muscle pain. *Dissertations Abstracts International: Section B: The Sciences and Engineering*, 57(6–8), 4038.

Ost, L. G. and Sterner, U. (1987). Applied tension: a specific behavioural method for treatment of blood phobia. *Behaviour Research and Therapy*, 25, 25–30.

Padesky, C. A. (1993). *Socratic Questioning: Changing Minds or Guided Discovery*. A keynote address given at the London Congress of The European Association of Behavioural and Cognitive Therapy.

Padesky, C. (1994). Schema change processes in cognitive therapy. *Clinical Psychology and Psychotherapy*, 1(5), 267–278.

Padesky, C. A. (1996). Developing cognitive therapist competency: teaching and supervision models. In Salkovskis, P. M. (ed.), *Frontiers of Cognitive Therapy*. New York: Guilford, pp. 266–292.

Padesky, C. A. and Greenberger, D. (1995). *Clinician's Guide to Mind over Mood*. New York: Guilford.

Pagliarulo, M. (2001). *Introduction to Physical Therapy*. Oxford: Mosby.

Persons, J. (1989). *Cognitive Therapy in Practice: A Case Formulation Approach*. New York: Norton.

Poulis, U. T. (1999). Alexithymia and chronic fatigue syndrome: A correlational self-report study. *Dissertation Abstracts International: Section B: The Sciences and Engineering*, 60(6-B), 2957.

Prins, J., Bleijenberg, G., Bazelmans, E., Elving, L., de Boo, T., Severens, H., van der Wilt, G., Spinhoven, P. and van der Meer, J. (2002). Cognitive behavior therapy for chronic fatigue syndrome: A multicenter randomized controlled trial. *Gedragstherapie*, 35(2), 165–180.

Raine, R., Carter, S., Sensky, T. and Black, N. (2004). General practitioners' perceptions of chronic fatigue syndrome and beliefs about its management, compared with irritable bowel syndrome: qualitative study. *British Medical Journal*, 328, 1354–1356.

Reiffenberger, D. H. and Amundson, L. H. (1996). Fibromyalgia syndrome: a review. *American Family Physician*, 53(5), 1698–1704.

Rosenstiel, A. K. and Keefe, F. J. (1983). The use of coping strategies in chronic low back pain patients. Relationship to patient characteristics and current adjustment. *Pain*, 17(1), 33–44.

Roth, P. and Fonagy, A. (1996). *What Works for Whom?* New York: Guilford.

Sanders, D. (1996). *Counselling for Psychosomatic Problems.* London: Sage.

Severens, J. L., Prins, I. B., van der Wilt, G. J., van der Meer, J. W. M. and Bleijenberg, G. (2004). Cost effectiveness of cognitive behavioural therapy for patients with chronic fatigue syndrome. *Quarterly Journal of Medicine*, 97(3), 156–161.

Sharoff, K. (2002). *Cognitive Coping Therapy.* London: Routledge.

Sharpe, M. and Chalder, M. (1994). Management of the chronic fatigue syndrome. *Neurological Rehabilitation.* Oxford: Oxford University Press.

Sharpe, M. C., Archard, L. C., Banatvala, J. E., Borysiewicz, L. K., Clare, A. W., David, A., et al (1991). A report on chronic fatigue syndrome: Guidelines for research. *Journal of the Royal Society of Medicine,* 84, 118–121.

Sharpe, M. C., Peveler, R. and Mayou, R. (1992). The psychological treatment of patients with functional somatic symptoms: a practical guide. *Journal of Psychosomatic Research,* 36(6), 515–529.

Sharpe, M. C., Hawton, K. E., Simkin, S., Sutawy, C., Klimes, I., Peto, T. E. A., Warrell, D. and Seagroatt, V. (1996). Cognitive therapy for chronic fatigue syndrome: a randomised controlled clinical trial. *British Medical Journal*, 312, 22–26.

Simos, G. (2002). *Cognitive Behaviour Therapy: A Guide for the Practising Clinician.* London: Brunner–Routledge.

Sims, A. (1993). *Symptoms in the Mind.* London: Bailliere Tindall.

Snell, C. R., Van Ness, J. M., Stevens, S. R., Phippen, S. G. and Dempsey, W. L. (2003). Exercise therapy. In Jason, L. A., Fennell, P. A. and Taylor, R. R. (eds) *Handbook of Chronic Fatigue Syndrome.* New York: Wiley, pp. 561–579.

Sullivan, M. J. and D'Eon, J. L. (1990). Relation between catastrophising and depression in chronic pain patients. *Journal of Abnormal Psychology*, 99, 260–263.

Surawy, C., Hackman, A., Hawton, K. and Sharpe, M. (1995). Chronic fatigue syndrome: a cognitive approach. *Behaviour Research and Therapy*, 33(5), 535–544.

Surawy, C., Roberts, J. and Silver, A. (2005). The effect of mindfulness training on mood and measures of fatigue, activity, and quality of life in patients with chronic fatigue syndrome on a hospital waiting list: A series of exploratory studies. *Behavioural and Cognitive Psychotherapy*, 33(1), 103–109.

Taillefer, S., Kirmayer, L. J., Robbins, J. M. and Lasry, J. C. (2003). Correlates of illness worry in chronic fatigue syndrome. *Journal of Psychosomatic Research*, 54(4), 331–337.

Talley, N. J. and Spiller, R. (2002). Irritable bowel syndrome: a little understood organic bowel disease? *Lancet,* 360, 555–564.

Teasdale, J. D., Segal, Z. V., Williams, J. M. G., Ridgeway, V. A., Soulsby, J. M. and Lau, M. A. (2000). Prevention of relapse/recurrence in major depression by mindfulness-based cognitive therapy. *Journal of Consulting and Clinical Psychology*, 68(4), 615–623.

Tiersky, A. T., Matheis, R. J., DeLuca, J., Lange, G. and Natelson, B. H. (2003). Functional status, neuropsychological functioning, and mood in chronic fatigue syndrome: relationship to psychiatric disorder. *Journal of Nervous and Mental Disease*, 191(5), 324–331.

Tiersky, L. A., Johnson, S. K., Lange, G., Natelson, B. H. and DeLuca, J. (1997). Neuropsychology of chronic fatigue: a critical review. *Journal of Clinical and Experimental Neuropsychology*, 19(4), 560–586.

Toner, B. B., Segal, Z. V., Emmott, S. D. and Myran, D. (2000). *Cognitive-Behavioral Treatment of Irritable Bowel Syndrome: The Brain-Gut Connection.* New York: Guilford.

Turk, D. and Ellis, B. (2003). Pain and fatigue. In Jason, A. J., Fennell, P. A., and Taylor R. R. (eds). *Handbook of Chronic Fatigue Syndrome.* New York: Wiley, pp. 211–244.

Unger, E. R., Nisenbaum, R., Moldofsky, H., Cesta, A., Sammut, C., Reyes, M., and Reeve, W. C. (2004). Sleep assessment in a population based study of chronic fatigue syndrome. *BMC Neurology*, 4, 6. http://www.biomedcentral.com/1471-2377/4/6. Accessed 8th November 2005.

Uslan, D. (2003). Rehabilitation counselling. In Jason, L.A., Fennell, P. A. and Taylor, R. R. (eds) *Handbook of Chronic Fatigue Syndrome*. New York: Wiley, pp. 654–692.

Van der Werf, S., Prins, J., Vercoulen, J. H., van der Meer, J. W. and Bleijenberg, G. (2000). Identifying physical activity patterns in chronic fatigue syndrome using actigraphic assessment. *Journal of Psychosomatic Research*, 49, 373–379.

Van Houdenhove, B., Onghena, P., Neerinckh, E. and Hellin, J. (1995). Does high action-proneness make people more vulnerable to chronic fatigue syndrome: a controlled psychometric study. *Journal of Psychosomatic Research*, 39, 633–640.

Van Konynenburg, R. A. (2003). Nutritional approaches. In Jason L. A., Fennell, P. A. and Taylor, R. R. (eds) *Handbook of Chronic Fatigue Syndrome*. New York: Wiley, pp. 580–653.

Vercoulen, J. H., Swanink, C. M., Zitman, F. G., Vreden, S. G., Hoofs, M. P., Fennis, J. F., et al (1996). Randomized, double-blind, placebo-controlled study of fluoxetine in chronic fatigue syndrome. *Lancet,* 347, 858–861.

Vita, P. and Owen, N. (1995). A perspective on the behavioural epidemiology, the determinants, and the stages of exercise involvement. *Australian Psychologist*, 30(2), 135–140.

Wagemaker, H. (1999). Chronic fatigue syndrome: The physiology of people on the low end of the spectrum of physical activity. *Clinical Science*, 97, 611–613.

Wearden, A. J., Morriss, R. K., Mullis, R., Strickland, P. L., Pearson, D. J., Appleby, L., Campbell, I. T. and Morris, J. A. (1998). Randomised, double-blind, placebo-controlled treatment trial of fluoxetine and graded exercise for chronic fatigue syndrome. *British Journal of Psychiatry,* 172(6), 485–490.

Wessely, S., David, A. S., Butler, S. and Chalder, T. (1989). Management of chronic (post viral) fatigue syndrome. *Journal of the Royal College of General Practitioners*, 39, 26–29.

Wessely, S., Hotopf, M. and Sharpe, M. (1998). *Chronic Fatigue and its Syndromes*. Oxford: Oxford University Press.

White, C. A. (2001). *Cognitive Behaviour Therapy for Chronic Medical Problems*. Chichester: Wiley.

White, C. and Schweitzer, R. (2000). The role of personality in the development and perpetuation of chronic fatigue syndrome. *Journal of Psychosomatic Research,* 48(6), 515–524.

White, P. D. and Naish, V. A. (2001). Graded movement therapy for chronic fatigue syndrome. *Physiotherapy,* 87(11), 614–616.

White, P. D., Thomas, J. and Amess, J. (1995). The existence of fatigue syndrome after glandular fever. *Psychological Medicine*, 25, 907–916.

White, P. D., Thomas, J. M., Kangro-Hillar, O., Bruce-Jones, W. D. A., Amess, J., Crawford, D. H., Grover-Shirlyn, A. and Clare, A. W. (2001). Predictions and associations of fatigue syndromes and mood disorders that occur after infectious mononucleosis. *Lancet*, 358, 1946–1954.

Whiting, P., Bagnall, A. M., Snowden, A. J., Cornell, J. E., Mulrow, C. D. and Ramirez, G. P. H. (2001). Interventions for the treatment and management of chronic fatigue syndrome: a systematic review. *Journal of the American Medical Association*, 286(11), 1360–1368.

Wills, F. and Sanders, D. (1997). *Cognitive Therapy: Transforming the Image*. London: Sage.

Wolfe, F., Smythe, H. A., Yunus, M. B., Bennet, R. M., Bombadier, C., Goldenberg, D. L., (1990). The American college of rheumatology 1990 criteria for the classification of fibromyalgia. Report of the multicentred criteria committee. *Arthritis and Rheumatism,* 33, 160–172.

Wood, B. and Wessely, S. (1999). Personality and social attitudes in chronic fatigue syndrome. *Journal of Psychosomatic Research*, 47(4), 385–397.

Young, J. E. (1994). *Cognitive Therapy for Personality Disorders: A Schema Focused Approach*. Sarasota, FL: Professional Resource Press.

Young, J. E. and Brown, G. (2001). *Young Schema Questionnaire: Special Edition*. New York: Schema Therapy Institute.

Young, J. E., Klosko, J., and Weishaar, M. E. (2003). *Schema Therapy: A Practitioner's Guide*. New York: Guilford.

Index